T0330525

Routledge Revivals

Farm Buildings

First published in 1983, *Farm Buildings* gives a fascinating account of what has been happening in and around farm buildings since medieval times, and describes their structure, their function and their style. This is followed by a long section in which sixty-eight representative types of Welsh and English farm buildings are commented on by the author and illustrated by John Penoyre. John Woodforde emphasizes that just as people increasingly enjoy looking at old farm buildings, so too some farmers are coming to appreciate them with a new eye, noting that they possess in their yards assets whose value is greater in several ways than they used to think. This book will be of interest to students of architecture, history and agriculture.

Farm Buildings
in England and Wales

John Woodforde

Routledge
Taylor & Francis Group

First published in 1983
By Routledge & Kegan Paul Ltd

This edition first published in 2023 by Routledge
4 Park Square, Milton Park, Abingdon, Oxon, OX14 4RN
and by Routledge
605 Third Avenue, New York, NY 10017

Routledge is an imprint of the Taylor & Francis Group, an informa business

© John Woodforde 1983

Publisher's Note
The publisher has gone to great lengths to ensure the quality of this reprint but points out that some imperfections in the original copies may be apparent.

Disclaimer
The publisher has made every effort to trace copyright holders and welcomes correspondence from those they have been unable to contact.

A Library of Congress record exists under ISBN: 071009275X

ISBN: 978-1-032-54207-2 (hbk)
ISBN: 978-1-003-41605-0 (ebk)
ISBN: 978-1-032-54269-0 (pbk)

Book DOI 10.4324/9781003416050

John Woodforde

Farm Buildings
in England and Wales

Sixty-eight types of farm structure
specially drawn by John Penoyre

Routledge & Kegan Paul
London, Boston, Melbourne and Henley

Under a higher degree of civilisation, conversion takes the place of destruction and things merely change their owners or their uses . . .

John Claudius Loudon,
Cottage, Farm and Villa Architecture, 1833

First published in 1983
by Routledge & Kegan Paul plc
39 Store Street, London WC1E 7DD,
9 Park Street, Boston, Mass. 02108, USA,
296 Beaconsfield Parade, Middle Park,
Melbourne, 3206, Australia, and
Broadway House, Newtown Road,
Henley-on-Thames, Oxon RG9 1EN
Set in 10 on 12 pt Ehrhardt by
Rowland Phototypesetting Ltd, Bury St Edmunds, Suffolk
and printed in Great Britain by
St Edmundsbury Press, Bury St Edmunds, Suffolk

Library of Congress Cataloging in Publication Data

Woodforde, John.

Farm buildings in England and Wales.
Bibliography: p.
Includes index.
1. Farm buildings – England – History. 2. Farm buildings
– Wales – History. 3. Farms – England – History.
4. Farms – Wales – History. 5. Agriculture – England
– History. 6. Agriculture – Wales – History. I. Title.
S787.G7W66 1983   631.2'0942   82-12359
ISBN 0-7100-9275-X

Contents

Chapter 9   SEVENTY YEARS OF NEGLECT

Effect of First World War – estates broken up afterwards – steadily deteriorating farmsteads – the contrast with new machines, engines and American structures – a successful farmer – few textbooks between 1880 and 1939 – tumbledown appearance of buildings a great attraction of the countryside in the 1930s – wartime's 'Make silage, make sure'

Chapter 10   THE REDUNDANT BARN

Useless barns of the early nineteenth century – a conversion to lodging house – well-liked landmarks in the landscape – the enterprise of Essex County Council – DOE listing of barns – a growing reluctance to demolish

PART TWO   EXAMPLES OF BUILDINGS

Acknowledgments

In being able to let loose this small book my main debts are to Mr Nigel Harvey, Mr John Penoyre, Mr Michael Hancock, the late John Claudius Loudon and the late Lord Ernle.

Mr Harvey, Honorary Librarian of the Royal Agricultural Society of England, has been concerned with farming all his life and, thanks to a Land-Lease consignment of heavy tractors, was one of the first to plough an acre in an hour. He trained as a land agent and worked for the Ministry of Agriculture, Fisheries and Food and for the Agricultural Research Council. His beautifully written *History of Farm Buildings in England and Wales*, is a standard work. I am grateful for his personal kindness to me and for checking my typescript.

Mr Penoyre is an architect as well as a writer on architectural matters and an illustrator. His drawings speak for themselves. Mr Hancock, a convert to farming after years in the City of London, suggested the book. His liking for old farm buildings, leading to a personal re-roofing of a barn, has been infectious.

Loudon is one of my heroes. His energetic and varied pursuits in life, despite ill health, command admiration while the voluminous nature of his writing, allowing for help from wife and paid professionals, often strikes me as superhuman. Others wrote practical books about farming – Waistell and Denton, for example – but none with the sense of the ridiculous which shines from so many of Loudon's sentences and makes them a joy to read. Further, farming was only one of his consuming interests.

Lord Ernle published *English Farming Past and Present* in 1912; it has since passed through several editions, the last appearing in 1961. It may now be considered dated in view of the findings of more recent research but it remains an extremely readable work in which nothing seems to have been left out. Lord Ernle's skill with a pen makes his writing hard to put down – I have consulted over 60 other books.

For photographic material kindly supplied for some of the drawings, I wish to thank Mr Roy Armstrong, the Arts Council, Atcost Ltd., Brent Central Library, the Corinium Museum, *Country Landowner, Country Life*, Mrs M. Coutin, Exeter University, Devonshire County Council, Fairley Local History Society, Mr and Mrs Michael Hancock, Miss M. Hartley, Mr Nigel Harvey, Mrs Rachel Hillier, the National Monuments Record, Lancashire County Council, Mr M. Michinson, Mr C. Murley, Mr and Mrs C. Moxon, Miss Pamla Toler, Mr Peter Turner, the Weald and Downland Museum and the Winchester City Museum.

John Woodforde

PART ONE

THE STORY BEHIND THE BUILDINGS

Chapter 1

Profiting from a Survival

The older farm buildings of England and Wales can be a delight to the eye of the ordinary person and sometimes, too, that of the farmer. But modern farm buildings can be in their way equally pleasing to look at. In any farmstead group half the buildings are well over a hundred years old and the others post-Second World War. There still exist around a million farm buildings put up before the last quarter of the nineteenth century – to judge by figures in the Hill and Kempson survey *Farm Buildings Capital* of 1977 – and, in an agricultural landscape of fewer hedges, trees and spinneys, they have never been more conspicuous, or more appreciated as records of former ways of farming.

Sheer adversity is in large measure the ironical reason for this vast legacy unmatched by that of other industries. For in the long period of the agricultural recession, starting in the 1870s, there was no money to demolish and renew, and buildings that became increasingly neglected had to go on serving their farms until the Second World War – farm buildings, apart from dairy buildings, which date from 1875 to 1945 are rarely seen. Many were spared again when building work became possible in the late 1940s because either they were found to be useful or not worth doing anything about; further, the new types of structure, which needed their own concrete foundations, could be put up alongside the old. Then came the conservation movement.

But, for economic reasons, the great period of adaptation was the 1950s. In the 1960s, when controls disappeared and money became easier, the bulldozer was often used: special-purpose buildings were more efficient than those built for another purpose and converted. Today there is a swing back to conversions, and farmers with a legacy of buildings from the past increasingly refuse to be embarrassed by them, seeking to repair and adapt rather than automatically order something new. Thus it is not hard to find farm stables sheltering milk-cooling equipment and granaries soft fruit and potatoes; ancient corn barns have regained a variety of agricultural functions such as housing combine harvesters, grain-dryers and workshop equipment; eighteenth-century cowhouses, with or without the original stalls, may actually contain cows on farms where loose housing is not the rule (an Agricultural Research Council pamphlet of 1960 reported the finding that loose-housed cows needed more grooming and more litter than cowhouse cows). Many farmers have taken the trouble to renovate with traditional materials, even going in for such cosmetic treatment as covering a concrete extension with weather-boards.

Most types of farm building are common to all parts of the country and differ in shape only according to the nature of the farming. A few, though, are seen in certain districts only: the primitive longhouses of the upland districts of the north and west in which people and animals were lodged together under the same roof; the bank barns characteristic of the Lake counties whose erection against a hillside makes possible an upper floor into which carts can be wheeled from ground level; the brick-and-tile looker's huts of Romney Marsh in Kent with a fireplace for shepherds; the ellum of the East Riding of Yorkshire, where a manger as well as a fireplace were a convenience for horses and ploughmen at break-times.

Differences arising from fashion, materials and craftsmanship are numerous and on view all over England. Once someone had devised a decorative feature, one by one his neighbours tended to copy it. Thus a Victorian estate owner in Cheshire, for example, decided to cheer up his stables with small round windows, or pitching holes, and before long small round windows enlivened stables for miles around. Farmers in the south-east vied with one another over the extent and handsomeness of the porches to corn barns, while in the Midlands and elsewhere porches were almost disregarded. Throughout the eastern counties the practices of the Netherlands, just across the North Sea, led to the forming of Dutch gables with tumbled brickwork.

Variety in building materials formerly followed local geology and in this, of course, farm buildings were in step with the smaller houses and cottages. (See *Houses in the Landscape*, 1978, a region-by-region study of the humbler building styles, by John Penoyre, illustrator of Part Two of this book, and Alec Clifton-Taylor's extensive work *The Pattern of English Building*.) Broadly speaking, in the highland areas buildings were made of hard stone, of timber or of brick, and in places where these were hard to come by they were made of earth – in Devon there are still plenty of old farm buildings with stout earth – chalk-and-straw – walls of the type known as cob – these need protection above and below from rain.

As for the different ways of putting the materials together, with wooden components especially, building traditions tend to have distinct territories: in points of construction buildings may differ not only between regions but even between one parish and the next. The details are easy to study in farm buildings because, unlike in houses, there is generally no concealment by plaster, rooms and passages.

In the west and parts of the north, barn builders were faithful to the age-old cruck system, setting pairs of timbers on the ground and securing them at the apex. Cut from naturally curving trees, these made a simple and effective framework from locally available materials, although they did limit the width. The spacing of about 16 feet (4.9m) between crucks is believed to be the origin of the bay – it was just wide enough to hold two pairs of oxen. In the east builders knew or practised

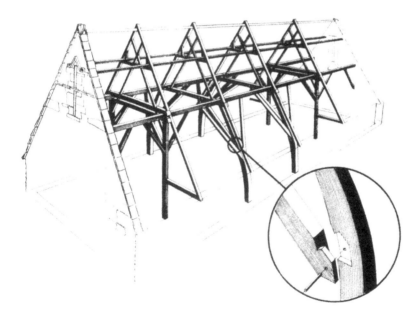

Timber framework of an early thirteenth-century barn at Siddington, Gloucestershire, showing a type of carpenter's joint peculiar to the period (C. A. Hewett, *Country Life*, 30 December 1971)

only the more sophisticated post-and-truss method of the Saxon noble-
man's house in which upright posts supported the roof. This construction allowed aisles at the sides where the roof slopes descended.

Both forms of framework can be compared with modern steel
frameworks in that no reliance is put on the walls, which are in fact
optional. Because of the care taken over joining the parts, the strength
and rigidity of old framed buildings in wood have often impressed
engineers.

The student of wooden framing finds himself in a world of scarf
joints, lap joints, king posts, crown posts and a hundred other early-
carpentry terms. Anyone entering a timber-framed barn comes to
understand how such men as Roy Armstrong, R. W. Brunskill, Richard
Harris and C. A. Hewett devoted years to the study of the intricacies of
timber construction of the past. Mr Hewett, through his exceptional
grasp of early wood joints, has been able to put forward a new date for
several famous buildings, and he has found a barn in Essex – at Paul's
Hall, Belchamp St Paul's – which contains a few timbers from before the
Norman Conquest – a finding apparently confirmed by a carbon dating
test (*Historic Barns*, 1979, p. 7). The short book by Richard Harris,
Discovering Timber-framed Buildings, 1978, offers a most readable introduction to a large but far from inaccessible subject.

At the beginning of the nineteenth century the craft disciplines under
which strong men turned 'trees into beams, into frames, into buildings'
(in the phrase of Mr Harris) came almost abruptly to an end. Everyone
was now praising brick, for which suitable brick earth was to be had on
most sites. But the mortar of those days did not contain cement, and

Design for a double barn, 1803 (*Rees' Encyclopaedia, Mansell
Collection*)

brick walls in fact relied on gravity to keep the bricks on top of one another. Brick storehouses, unlike locked-together timber storehouses, were often unequal to the lateral thrust of the crops piled up inside. For the elegant brick barns built at Holkham at the end of the eighteenth century there were special instructions about loading to reduce the risk of burst walls (J. C. Loudon's *Encyclopaedia of Agriculture*, 1831): some walls did give way and, like those of less-imposing barns, have had to be held together with steel tie rods.

With the coming of canals and then railways, and their usefulness in conveying hitherto local building materials like slate to all parts of the land, those who put up farm buildings came to rely less and less on the materials to hand; in due course bricks and iron trusses could be delivered wherever they were wanted. Many excellent farm buildings were built in the prosperous years of farming of the mid-Victorian period, and whether they are in Kent or Lancashire they may closely resemble one another.

Complete and barely altered farmsteads from the old days, whether Victorian, Georgian or earlier, are now rare, but there are plenty whose former completeness in layout, and the interdependence of the various parts, is discernible through the building work which has been added. For what it was like to be a labourer, one of many, living and working in the farmsteads of the past – so charming to look at on a summer's day and largely freed now of teeming rats, mice and fleas – information can be had from at least a few first-hand accounts.

The object of this book, however, is to consider how the farm buildings admired by visitors to the countryside came into existence, and how far that admiration is shared by farmers whose normal business is to make money by producing as much food as possible. Does it cost the public food to keep the buildings as the public wants them, or is there a happy mean whereby the interests of farmer and viewer can merge? To end this chapter in a personal manner, I can say that farmer neighbours, having secured an adequate living, are certainly conscious of appearances and of the reaction of others to their working environment.

Chapter 2

Growing Rich on Sheep

In the prehistoric times of, say, three thousand years ago, it appears that there existed hardly any farm buildings as we think of them. A man's hut, defensively constructed and often circular, sheltered in its single room not only his family but also his produce and animals. The latter would have been a comfort on a cold evening since a cow offers roughly the heat of a one-bar electric fire. For animals in quantity, pens were formed (cattle are indigenous, sheep were introduced in the late Stone Age, pigs were roaming boars). The pens had walls of stone or earth round them, and archeologists now say that some of the ancient upland earthworks are the remains not of forts but of cattle enclosures.

Much later on the Romans arrived and farmed with the aid of elaborate villa complexes. When they withdrew after four hundred years their villas gradually became quarries for building materials, and Saxon farmers went back to an old Celtic type of farmstead which concentrated everything under its one thatched roof. The typical building was small and had a central threshing floor with a storage loft above. On one side of this floor lay the farmer's quarters with partitions for women and on the other stalls for oxen and horses. The construction generally depended on crucks, the pairs of trees set in the ground to form arches. The Danish invaders, who were equally glad to have everything in one building, put up rather larger timber halls, with internal pillars and much subdivision. Norsemen and later the Normans preferred, if well-to-do, not to live at close quarters with farm animals and drove them out to adjacent shelters.

By the eleventh century there were manorial lords who lived in a quite civilized way, according to an early eleventh-century book on estate management called the *Gerefa*. The house of an estate owner, it was recommended, should be equipped with buildings round a court, and in that court there should be such things as ovens, kilns, a salthouse and a malthouse. The barn should be the hub of the place. Over a hundred implements are enumerated in the *Gerefa* for use in the barn and in those apartments where such work as food preparation, shoemaking and spinning took place (P. H. Blair, *Anglo-Saxon England*, 1956).

The *Domesday Book* survey, compiled for taxation purposes between 1085 and 1086, shows that self-contained estates called manors were sprinkled over England – generally separated from one another by dense woodland. But while the lord of the manor had rooms that were free of cattle and manure, the inhabitants of the villages and hamlets endured, as ever, a rude and earthy life: tenants, and a few freed men, clustered in shacks of wood, turf or clay, sharing the one room with livestock. (Within living memory crofters have had cows join them by the fireside circle and found milk yield improved by the warmth.)

During the five hundred years that followed *Domesday*, the techniques of arable farming hardly changed. In that period, though, the horse gradually began its career as a farm animal – there is a Suffolk record of horses being harnessed to ploughs early in the twelfth century – but the ox, slow, steady and in the end edible, remained the main source of drawing power. (A few teams of oxen were still working the land in Sussex in the early twentieth century.)

Oxhouses had extra wide doorways for the big horns. In a manorial record of the thirteenth century reference is made to an oxhouse 33 feet long and 12 feet wide on an estate at Kensworth in Hertfordshire, and a fourteenth-century document describes a shed at Rothley in Leicester-shire which quartered 24 oxen, 11 cows, 9 bullocks, 4 calves and a bull. Pigs were considered woodland animals and commonly had no special shelter provided for them.

Only traces remain of medieval farmsteads, for buildings of wood, clay and straw easily crumble back into the soil. The few medieval barns which have survived have done so because they were not ordinary, and were built of stone. As for the splendidly solid tithe barns on former monastic estates in the west, these, as Nigel Harvey has said in his *History of Farm Buildings*, 1970, were hardly farm buildings at all; they represented ecclesiastical wealth and were central storage depots of huge agricultural estates, housing the harvests of scattered farms and such dues and rents as were paid in kind. The medieval dovecotes were not ordinary buildings of the farm, either. Fashioned since Norman times in a variety of shapes, their function was to provide the privileged with fresh meat in the winter when livestock had been slaughtered for lack of feed; it made a pleasant change from salt beef. Dovecotes were home for thousands of pigeons living off the surrounding fields, and were much complained about; but although permitted only for lords of manors, the number of dovecotes grew until, in the seventeenth century, England was reckoned to have about 26,000.

The first book on farming to be printed in England was the *Boke of Husbondrye*, 1523, by Sir Anthony Fitzherbert, a farmer in Derbyshire. Among his detailed instructions for the year's work there is scarcely a mention of farm buildings, but he does describe how corn ricks should be raised on a scaffold to keep away vermin. (This precaution has always been largely disregarded, and a steam-threshing contractor recently recalled in conversation with Michael Winstanley: 'You'd catch as many as 80 rats a day out of a rick' – *Life in Kent*, 1978.)

Fitzherbert believed in enclosed farms as being more efficient than the open kind where several villagers shared unfenced strips, and he observes, as many have observed since, that 'an housbande cannot thrive well by his corne without he have cattell, or by his cattell without corne'. He was by no means the first to explain that of all animals the sheep could be the most profitable. Chaucer, in *The Canterbury Tales*, puts these animals at the top of a list of his Reeve's responsibilities:

His lordes sheepe, his neet, his dayerye,
His swyn, his hors, his stoor and his pultrye,
Was hoolly in this reves governyng. . . .

Bred primarily for their wool, sheep were also taken seriously as milk producers, and dairies existed for turning ewe's milk into butter and cheese. In view of the present-day talk about housing sheep in the winter, it is of interest to find that buildings were being put up in the thirteenth century to give protection between 'Martinmass and Easter'. This was done mainly in upland districts, but in 1352 the monks at Battle Abbey built a sheephouse in a lowland part, and it was 100 ft long and 14 ft wide (R. Trow-Smith, *A History of British Livestock Husbandry*).

Although enthusiastic about sheep, Fitzherbert certainly did not recommend keeping them in enormous quantities to the exclusion of everything else. This is exactly what some people were already doing, and it so happened that shortly after the appearance of his book it became a craze. Landowners and yeomen farmers realized that instead of employing bands of men to cultivate their ground they could grow rich by turning on to it hundreds of sheep, to be looked after by a single shepherd.

By various means, considerable tracts of land, especially in the Midlands, were taken over as sheep runs; tenants and cottagers were evicted, villages became deserted and farm buildings were in some cases actually destroyed as a signal that normal farming in that district was over. Although this destruction was after a time forbidden – the government had become alarmed by the decline in crop-growing and by rural depopulation – it was easy to stay within the law by keeping a single room for the shepherd or milkmaid.

Protests from the evicted, and from men in high positions on their behalf, made a big noise. There were several parts of the country where these lines written by Thomas Bastard in 1598 had relevance:

Sheepe have eate up our medows and our downes,
Our Corne, our wood, whole villages and townes.

Rural distress led to much stealing and to attempts by the owners of horses, sheep and poultry to fortify the places where they were kept. The most serious of several protests was the one known as Kett's Rising in Norfolk in 1549, during which peasants who had gathered in force on Mousehold Heath slaughtered 20,000 sheep.

The enclosing and sheep-grazing movement continued throughout Queen Elizabeth's reign: its decline, and that of the ruthless destruction of dwellings that went with it, came at last not so much because of any legislative action as because of such economic causes as a drop in the price of wool and a rise in that of corn. With some exceptions, farmers in the seventeenth century respected a sensible balance between tillage and pasture.

Meanwhile most who had to do with sheep grew rich. The proceeds from wool largely account for a wholesale rebuilding of rural England between about 1565 and the beginning of the seventeenth century. Wool merchants helped to build parish churches and are commemorated in memorial brasses, other tradesmen modernized their houses, and William Harrison, Essex contributor to *Holinshed's Chronicle*, recorded in 1577 that villagers marvelled to see 'the multitude of brick chimnies lately erected'.

A primitive type of rural building being used in Elizabethan times (it was still being built in parts remote from the up-to-date south-east) was the combined farmhouse and stockhouse under a sweeping roof of thatch. The type was timber-framed with two aisles, or outshots, and contained stalls for animals with lofts above them. S. O. Addy in *Evolution of the English House*, 1933, thought it probable that 'in many of these houses, the men slept above the stalls in one aisle and women above the stalls in the other' (where both groups would have benefited at times from the warmth coming from the large bodies below). Such houses, where anything remains of them, have now been altered beyond recognition.

Of the best farmsteads put up in the building boom of the late sixteenth century much is known, as they are still to be seen. It is known, for example, that although all Elizabethan farmers kept meats, crops and dairy products under the family roof, it was always found preferable in lowland eastern districts to have the house separate from the livestock buildings, even if only a few feet away. (This was to become traditional in English farming, unlike in Italian farming.) The house was gabled; it had an oak frame in all parts of the country except those where cob (earth) construction was established – as in the south-west – or where stone was especially easy to obtain; it faced north-east in the expectation of avoiding plague germs thought to be brought on south winds. Separate from equally gabled and detached outhouses, the collection formed three sides of a rectangle with a yard in the middle.

The inventory taken in 1585 of the estate of William Cullinge, a yeoman with probably about 100 acres on the downs of Kent, shows that in addition to his house he had a hay barn and also a wheat barn; and there were lofts in which he stored further quantities of corn. He kept 73 sheep, but need never have feared popular reprisals, since his farm was demonstrably mixed and by no means just a sheep run: he had 5 cows and 6 horses and grew fodder for them. On such a farm, sheep had a manurial value on top of that reposing in their wool, meat and milk: by rotation their droppings could enrich the soil for corn-growing, a cycle known as sheep-and-corn husbandry.

A farmer could make a modest living even today with a strictly Elizabethan farmstead as his base – especially if there was a barn where large vehicles and a corn-dryer could be put. Ralph Whitlock has made a study of an Elizabethan farmstead in Essex which was in fact still functioning unaltered until the 1950s. The buildings, he writes, in *A Short History of Farming*, 1965, were thatched and had a wooden framework filled in with wattle and plaster. One wing of the rectangle contained a dairy, a washhouse and an earth closet; the other wing contained the stable, cowhouse and cartshed. A granary stood alone in a cobbled yard. These outbuildings were so thoughtfully disposed round the dwelling-house, Mr Whitlock says, that the farmer 'lieing in his bed [a contemporary is quoted] may lightlie heare what is doone in each of them with ease, and call quicklie to his meine if anie danger should attack him.'

In the highland zones especially, simple farmhouses went on being built with one roof to shelter people, produce, animals and fowls: they looked like a terrace of single-storey cottages and were arranged in two intercommunicating sections. The often-quoted statistician Gregory King, writing about Cheshire with the help of the hearth tax in 1696, said that many farmers still 'had their fire in the midst of the house, against a hob of clay, and their oxen under the same roof.'

The farmer's quarters in these so-called longhouses usually consisted of one room, with box beds, for all purposes. But that sufficed quite acceptably. When the animals were moved elsewhere, as happened increasingly in the seventeenth century, the nether end of the house – it was so called in Yorkshire – was seldom taken in for domestic purposes. There was always the feeling, as M. W. Barley has said in *The English Farmhouse*, 1961, that the driven-out cattle might have to be brought back in a hard winter; so the nether end became a mere service room, a shelter for sheep bars, troughs and fuel.

The story of the longhouses of Devon, serving generations of farmers, is especially well documented. Traditionally these buildings had their nether ends stoutly separated from the living quarters by a stone wall, though access to the animals was direct through a door in that wall. It opened on to a sort of cross-walk within the cattlehouse by means of which the animals entered from the yard. A common seventeenth-century improvement was to build another wall, usually in the form of a light partition, which turned the cross-walk into an enclosed cross-passage; now the farmer had two doors and a lobby between his living room and the cattle. The building of longhouses was forbidden as unhygienic by most local authorities in the 1920s, but even in 1980 a few on Dartmoor took in animals, as well as people, during severe weather.

A new scientific interest in agriculture during the seventeenth century is evident from the broadening flow of books and pamphlets which were issued, several of them from the Royal Society. An improved version of the age-old treadmill crane for raising water must be mentioned on account of the admiration it drew. A small animal like a donkey treading inside a large wheel could raise bucket after bucket from a great depth. But in the end the principle was to be of less significance than wheels turned horizontally – by horses, wind, water and steam – which were developed in the eighteenth century.

Hops, first introduced on any scale from the Netherlands in the previous century, were considered a farm crop to be cultivated in quantity and processed to form an ingredient in beer-making; those who had tried the new kind of beer were agreed that dried hop flowers made the liquor from malted barley more agreeable to the eye and actually pleasant to the taste. The period saw the equipment of barn-like sheds for drying hop flowers by means of fires lit beneath them – they were dried, too, in malt kilns, and slowly in attics without artificial heat. But the oasthouses which appear regularly in inventories from the south-east pass unnoticed today through not having the kiln tower which became the rule a hundred and fifty years later in Kent.

As a few of the towns grew bigger, so a difficulty arose of supplying them, without refrigeration or fast transport, with milk from the country. The urban cowhouse, for all its drawbacks, seemed the only answer, and thus farm buildings began to establish themselves, unhygienically, in the streets of London and elsewhere.

Those concerned with putting up the basic farm buildings of the mixed farm proceeded without a thought about new designs. No one saw any need for change. Nigel Harvey writes that in the textbook of 1727 by Edward Laurence, *The Duty and Office of a Land Steward*, the only specific reference to farm buildings was a suggestion that they should be roofed with slates or tiles instead of straw, partly to reduce the risk of fire and partly to save straw for making manure. Laurence was like his predecessors and contemporaries in assuming, as Nigel Harvey has commented, that a mixture of common sense, traditional lore and access to locally arising building materials would enable any landowner or farmer to furnish his land with satisfactory buildings.

Slates from North Wales were of course local only in a few districts and the necessary carriage utterly discouraged their general employment, and to an extent that of tiles. Only if there was access to a suitable waterway was it feasible to procure building materials from a distance. Even in London the road between Kensington and Mayfair was said in the 1730s to be an impassable gulf of mud. In the rural districts the dreadful state of the roads often stopped all winter carriage-traffic, forced villages and hamlets to be self-sufficient and led to the building of numerous small barns. Often these had no door wide enough to admit a small cart, let alone a loaded hay waggon. It was not that no one wanted to wheel things in, just that in some villages, especially villages in hilly areas, any kind of wheeled vehicle was almost unknown: crops were brought home by pack-horses and flour dragged from the mill through ancient ruts.

Chapter 3

The Granary of Europe

In the seventeenth century there were plenty of self-employed yeoman farmers – and tenant farmers, too – who were independent in that they had control over the land they worked. But until well into the eighteenth century most farming was still done on medieval lines in open-field areas and involved a complicated partnership with villagers amid strips of land. The farmers' houses and farm buildings were inconveniently squeezed together in the villages and might be two miles from the land they served, an arrangement which entailed not only much travelling but also in season the carrying to and fro of crops and manure.

The old open-field farm comprised two or three fenced arable areas divided without any substantial barrier into a number of strips in different parts of the large fields. After two harvests, perhaps one of wheat and one of barley, each of the great fields was given a rest during which it was grazed by the parish sheep and cattle. Other village livestock, normally populating the commons, was allowed to graze on the stubble and also on any marshy or hilly unploughed land which the fields might contain. Each farmer was allotted a share of grassland for cutting some hay and each had grazing rights on the village green. Determined by communal law and custom, the open-field system is exemplified to this day at the much visited village of Laxton in Nottinghamshire, the only place in Britain where the system is still in existence.

Apart from the unnecessary journeys and confusion about the boundaries of the strips, an objection raised to this kind of farming was that a man could not grow turnips as winter feed because everyone's cows were driven into the field as soon as the harvests were in, and that he could not improve his animals because they mixed with the animals of others.

Where the system was from time to time brought to an end, grazing rights were taken away and the scattered ploughland strips and open communal grazings re-allocated to form compact farms under the control of one person, for whom they were divided into the sort of fields that can still be seen. The change was called enclosure. It often brought with it the termination of grazing rights on greens and commons, these being divided among individual occupiers – usually tenants – and fenced into fields. Permission to make an enclosure often caused distress through depriving peasants of rights to the use of small pieces of ground – and depriving them, too, of a meagre independent livelihood.

But the effect on the development of farmsteads was good: Georgian farm buildings are nearly all results of the Enclosure Movement. The

 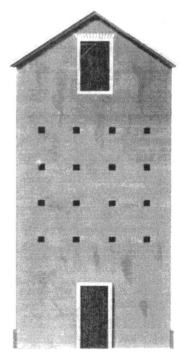

Granary, 1814 (*Rees' Enclopaedia, Mansell Collection*)

lucky enclosing landlord, who may have fought for his permission to enclose, was free to exercise his own taste in preparing new hedged holdings complete with a centrally placed farmhouse and farmery; he was free, of course, to make his own choice of a tenant farmer, whose sole management of the newly laid-out farm encouraged efficient farming.

Equipped with a full range of buildings, many of these tenant farmers found that with hard work there was a lot of money left over after paying the rent. Newly prosperous farmers in eastern England were noted by Jean le Blanc at the beginning of what has been called the eighteenth century's golden age of farming. He wrote in *Letters on the English and French Nations*, 1747: 'The English farmer is rich and enjoys all the conveniences of life in abundance . . . it is a pity that this plenty which he enjoys should make him so proud and insolent.' But it must be added that other travellers said the opposite about the typical English farmer.

The fencing of commons and the breaking up of open-field farms had been going on slowly, and generally without recourse to law, for about three hundred years. After the mid-eighteenth century the enclosing process accelerated. So profitable was it seen to be that many landlords sought to get what they wanted through a private Act of Parliament; this course nearly always led to the overruling of objections by private proprietors. In the period 1740–60, 156 Enclosure Acts were passed and in the period 1790–1800, no less than 506. The argument calculated to impress the authorities was that more food was needed for a growing population.

Farmers who were encouraged by enthusiastic landlords did indeed increase the country's production of food, as gradually more scientific methods of working were taken up. Several men helped greatly by their example. Jethro Tull, author of *The New Horse-Houghing Husbandry*, 1731, introduced new crops and demonstrated the advantages of drilling wheat and roots in rows, so that the growing plants could be hoed. Lord Townshend, legendary promoter of the turnip, and one of the land-owners who was also a practical farmer, showed how light and sandy soil could be improved by treatment with marl and clay, and he popular-ized the so-called Norfolk system of cropping whereby cereals, roots and artificial grasses were alternated. Some of those who imitated him made fortunes.

Thomas Coke of Holkham introduced the use of artificial foods like oil cake to supplement roots as winter feed for animals, and he made wheat grow where none would do so before. Robert Bakewell of

Leicestershire revolutionized stockbreeding by mating not merely animals of the same breed but also of the same family: his fleshy sheep and oxen and his active, muscular carthorses became famous. A bachelor, he would entertain in his farmhouse kitchen – Lord Ernle wrote in *English Farming Past and Present*, 1912 – British peers, Russian princes and French and German dukes as well as sightseers from all over England.

By the 1790s the livestock sold at Smithfield Market in London were almost unrecognizably larger than the livestock sold there at the beginning of the century. This addition to the country's meat supply, for which Bakewell was in large measure responsible, would not have been possible without enclosed farms. On open-field farms and commons, a lack of breeding control, of winter keep and adequate shelter caused the livestock to be, in comparison, dwarfs.

English agriculture was fortunate, too, during the latter part of the eighteenth century in the work of Arthur Young as a spreader of information. Although himself a failed farmer, he worked untiringly as a traveller and writer for what he believed to be the progress of good farming. In his fluently written and pithy *Tours* of England, for which he secured interviews with thousands of farmers, he circulated news of experiments under way, research, statistics and notes of the useful practices and new methods which he had encountered. In 1784 he started a monthly magazine called *Annals of Agriculture* which continued until 1809. George III, an eager reader of Young's writings, contributed occasionally to the magazine under the name of his shepherd at Windsor, Ralph Robinson.

England's population doubled during the eighteenth century and the number of horses trebled; yet as a result of agricultural changes the country's food was produced from within her own boundaries. Given the badness of roads everywhere, London could have become a problem as the number of inhabitants approached a million; but the seventeenth-century urban cowhouses increased in numbers and size, and pigs were now being farmed intensively in the capital by brewers and distillers glad of fattening houses as an outlet for starchy waste products. Meanwhile national grain yields were good enough in some years for Lord Ernle to write of England as 'the granary of Europe'.

The actual granaries on their staddle stones to keep away rats were alarmingly full in season, especially in southern England. Some farmers stored grain additionally in barns, which were inclined to bulge under the thrust, and needed strengthening at times; other farmers stored it in lofts over cowhouses, stables or cartsheds, the latter having the advantage, it was said, that there was no foul air to rise up from animals.

Most of these buildings, despite normal incentives to repair or build afresh, had become prematurely decrepit. Farmers tended to be sparing with straw for roofing purposes, the prevalence of wispy thatching being reflected in contemporary paintings of rural scenes. The standard of the nation's farm buildings in no way reflected the improvement in production. It was in general only on the enclosed estates of landowners who took a personal interest in appearance, or aspired – for their own use – to the fashionable *ferme ornée*, that sound new buildings appeared – perhaps made with bricks baked from clay on the site. These are the Georgian farm buildings, and complete farmsteads, of which so many have survived, with accretions, to be seen and admired today. Arthur Young in his book *On the Present State of the Waste Lands*, 1773, remarks that some members of the landed gentry were beggared in their efforts to rival the rural building activities of neighbours who had made fortunes through trades other than farming.

By the 1750s, independent farmers, those who had formerly been called yeomen, were few; in Nigel Harvey's words, 'the landlord and tenant system now dominated the countryside' and the varied arrangements of former times were being largely exchanged for a basis on which

Octagonal farmstead in Picturesque manner, 1831.
Note stack yard and smaller barn (J. C. Loudon, *Encyclopaedia of Agriculture*)

the landlord, in return for a cash rent, provided the land and the buildings which the tenant made use of. Robert Bakewell was unusual as a tenant farmer in putting up stalls at his own expense. And very good they were, with a platform for the cows nicely calculated for dung to fall beyond the edge. Farm buildings had become an interesting responsibility of the landowners and of the agents and designers appointed to help them, and the planning and construction of such buildings was a constant topic in the pamphlets, manuals, and accounts of agricultural travel which in this period competed for the attention of the landed gentry.

To look through the architects' pattern books of the second half of the eighteenth century, the period of the Agricultural Revolution, is to find that the few farm-building pages were devoted to ornamental designs. No building received more decorative treatment than the dairy, which had formerly crouched to one side of the farmhouse. However, the architects' audience is clear from the opening words of his section on dairies in John Papworth's *Rural Residences* (1818): 'When the fashionable amusements of the town are relinquished for those of the country, there

Dairy at Woburn Abbey, 1809 (*Rees' Encyclopaedia, Mansell Collection*)

are few so interesting to the female mind as the dairy. . . .' His picture of a dairy shows a kind of thatched summer house.

This was the age of the *ferme ornée* – or the idea of it – in which architect-designed buildings reflected a preoccupation with the picturesque and for landscapes which resembled paintings of landscapes. In a *ferme ornée* farm buildings had the look of decorative structures for the garden and even the humble roothouse was given a new face to please the eye. Among several references to roothouses in his book *The Picturesque*, 1927, Christopher Hussey wrote that the proprietor of an estate near Chertsey in Surrey had been persuaded to enliven a winding path with a roothouse, a Gothic temple and a menagerie.

Fermes ornées, in which the buildings might present semi-circles, polygons and designs in the Gothic, Rustic or Chinese taste, were indeed rarely considered for tenant farmers; the architects were seeking the patronage of landowners concerned about the look of their home farm – that is, the farm within their park. Such landowners tended to think that buildings, and certainly plain buildings, were an intrusion on the prospect offered by parkland; and some of the ornamental buildings of the literature were actually put up: a castellated cowhouse by William Kent at Rousham, Oxfordshire, and another of crescent shape at Burn Hall, Durham are among various famous examples given in the *National Trust Book of the Farm*, 1981, by Gillian Darley.

To unite a park with a farm was very difficult, said the landscape gardener Humphrey Repton, the one being 'the object of beauty and the other of profit'. Typically of those who were self-confident in the Georgian age, rich landowners were sometimes prepared to raise earth banks rather than see from the windows of their houses the economic basis of their estates, even when it consisted of buildings designed by a selected architect.

Thomas Coke of Holkham was a good example of a landowner who spent money freely but not extravagantly on equipping farms, and so was the Duke of Bedford at Woburn, Lord Egremont at Penshurst and dozens of others. Coke's farm buildings, farmhouses and cottages – all English-classical in style – were models of their period; they cost him, according to Lord Ernle, half a million eighteenth-century pounds. By offering leases longer than other people offered – twenty-one years – Coke got his tenants to look after the buildings in their own interest, and to divert labour to improve them.

Chapter 4

Cows without Cowhouses

Arthur Young in his *Tours* often urged farmers to renew their farm buildings completely. He and his rival agricultural pundit, William Marshall – another compulsive writer – had in mind as the ideal plan an all-purpose farmyard with a concentration of livestock and stored produce at a centre next to the house. This was now permitted to face south with its back to the farmyard. From the barn should go fodder and litter for the cattle; from the cattle, manure for the crops and milk to the dairy; from the dairy, buttermilk and whey to the piggeries. (Today there are other cycles. A Dorset pig farmer, for instance, described in 1980 how from his pigs went dung for the meadows, from the meadows went grass for making into cubes, from the cube factory came food for the pigs.) Arthur Young had to travel many miles behind a horse to find a mixed farm operating in a way he thought sensible, and after a tour of Norfolk he reported that he 'did not see one good farmstead in the country'.

An easy mixer but quickly indignant, he was scornful of backward practices, and writing about Buckinghamshire and Northamptonshire in the 1770s, he described tersely a custom of daubing the walls of farm buildings with 'lumps of cow dung mixed with short straw', to be used when dry as fuel. 'There cannot', said Young, 'be such an application of manure anywhere but among Hottentots.' He referred in the same year to cows without cowhouses, carts without shelters and steadings without central yards.

In 1793 Pitt established the Board of Agriculture, with Arthur Young as its secretary, and one of its first undertakings was to appoint commissioners to collect information on the state of farming in each county. They set out with high standards and encouragement to look critically on the buildings of farms which were not orderly in appear-

ance. Most of their reports are interspersed with remarks about hap-
hazard arrangement.

In Middlesex the farm buildings were said to be as a rule 'erected
piecemeal'; in Monmouthshire they were 'scattered about at random'; in
Cornwall the barns and the houses for cows and oxen 'stood about in
confusion' and in Oxfordshire even the stone buildings were 'wretched-
ly contrived and executed'. The report from Somerset said that 'on all
the dairy farms a shameful inattention prevails in respect to outhouses
and sheds for the stock to retire to in the winter months'; cattle were

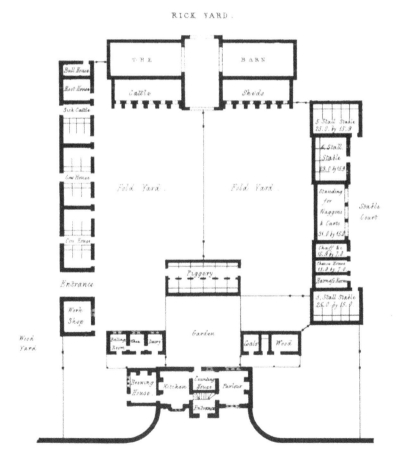

Farmstead plan, 1830 (Peter Robinson, *Design for Farm
Buildings*)

almost universally served with their provender in the open field, with the result that not enough manure was collected from twenty of them to fertilize an acre of arable land.

From county after county there was criticism about the position of farmhouses, many of which were in villages at a distance from their farms. The reporter for Devon, a man called Vancouver, remarked: 'We defy ingenuity to plan and place farmhouses worse.' He noted with disapproval that the cob-built garden walls, farmhouses, barns, stables, lime kilns, fences and cottages were 'built without roughcast or whitewash to conceal the native colour of the loam'.

Essex was among the counties where the farm buildings made a good impression – 'numerous and convenient; many expensive rick shelters and barns'. Northumberland, later to become a famous wheat-growing area, was another; it had good examples of farmeries showing 'the improved manner of distributing the various offices on the East, West and North sides of a rectangle'. Lancashire had many farm buildings without order or design, but some new ones were noted which had been erected 'to the most approved plans'.

Individual buildings were described for emulation: Lord Egremont's semi-circular piggery at Petworth in Sussex, Lord Penrhyn's colonnaded poultry house at Winnington in Cheshire; but some fort-like

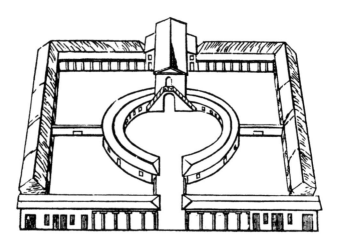

Design for a corn and stall-feeding farm, 1844. Note stacks built over stables and sheds (J. C. Loudon, *Encyclopaedia of Agriculture*)

pigsties in Shropshire were mentioned only as artifacts to be avoided, 'objectionable because they are intended to deceive'. One of Lord Ernle's comments on the mass of evidence provided by the commissioners is that in various respects there were landlords who had yet to be taught the business of owning and letting land. 'Goths and vandals' existed 'not only among tenants but also among owners.'

However inconvenient the state of most of the nation's farm buildings, agriculture was an unexpectedly profitable business in the period 1780 to 1815 – that is, up to the end of the Napoleonic wars. Being any sort of farmer, as distinct from a worker on the land, became a sought-after career, and in contrast to the situation in, say, the 1770s, when numerous small farmers were forced out by enclosures and amalgamations, there now emerged a new body of smallholders with tiny mixed farms. The headquarters of such people generally consisted of a brick or stone box, with a single room below for cattle and another above for the family, the latter entering and leaving by an outside stair to avoid having to go past the animals. The eighteenth-century bank barn, nestling against a hillside in the Lake District, might contain living accommodation.

At the same time, though, low wages and high prices for provisions in the late eighteenth century brought great hardship to all kinds of farm worker, many of whose cottages, even on rich men's estates, were worse than farm buildings; and life was almost intolerable for the bands of peasants and labourers deprived by enclosure of access to commons or a plot of land, and rarely able to pick up a few days' work – it is not surprising that a poor man would poach rabbits and risk deportation to Australia.

Already keen about new developments in the technique of agriculture, which made much talk in fashionable circles, some landowners were spurred to fresh exertions and outlays of capital by the large returns on their expenditure. It is no accident of history that some of the best country houses were built or improved at this time.

The artisan class was growing fast and the great need was more corn for bread. Several kinds of new crops were sown and better ploughs introduced. Meikle's threshing machine of 1784 began to supersede the hand flailers – abolishing unhealthy but welcome winter piece-work in the barns; winnowing machines took over from the wind as chaff-removers; such mechanical aids as chaff-cutters and turnip-slicers appeared; here and there, vast sums of money were spent on farm buildings.

In spite of the increased efforts leading to generally higher produc-

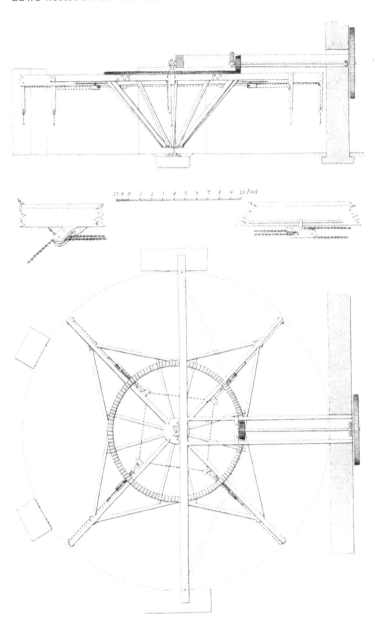

Mechanism for a horse wheel for four horses, 1844
(Henry Stephens, *The Book of the Farm*)

tion, prices never stopped getting higher and taking rents with them. They did so mainly because of the effect of a heavy sprinkling of bad seasons on a nation which was practically dependent on home-grown supplies: a mere partial failure in crops caused panic and talk of the prospect of dearth. In 1782 an import of wheat was resorted to which amounted to over half the home production. Even straw was imported – from Germany.

Meanwhile the open arable farms were being broken up and enclosed as soon as Acts of Parliament allowed, while virgin tracts of land were energetically reclaimed for wheat-growing; for such was the good return from farming that the least-productive fields were tilled at a profit by farmers well able to pay their rent to the owners.

With the French wars of 1793 to 1814 came inability to import at will and still more prosperity for farmers; there was apprehension of famine and prices rose to crippling heights. During those years, fourteen below-standard harvests affected the whole of Europe and little grain was available from America. There was a respite in the years 1808 and 1809 when the northern part of the Continent had good harvests and, at the height of the war with Napoleon, England was able, extraordinarily, to get extra supplies from the cornfields of France.

As landlords and farmers became ever richer and laughed about Napoleon being the patron saint of agriculture, the condition of the farm labourers amounted to a national disaster and one that was made much of by the reforming writers: Crabbe, Cobbett, Kent and John Wood junior, to mention only a few. Even milk was hard to find in the country. It seems that instead of selling at the farmhouse door what they had left over after supplying town customers, the farmers, were giving it along with whey to their pigs in the pen-and-run sties where fattening for the towns took place.

It was hard for the rural poor to find fuel. Even stretches of growing hedge disappeared and farmers with dry stone walls round their fields congratulated themselves on the incombustible nature of their barriers. Because of enclosures the commons, on which fuel had formerly been collected for nothing, were now out of bounds. In the 1790s a writer in the *Annals of Agriculture* suggested that the rural poor should take to the stables for warmth, as was apparently the practice in the duchy of Milan; fewer would suffer death from want of fuel, he argued, and throwing open the numberless stables would be a way of helping people without cost, cattle being 'so obliging as to dispense with warmth from their persons for nothing'. Although the scheme was not adopted, it is known that farmers with a permanent staff of farm servants liked to have the unmarried ones sleeping in lofts above byres, oxhouses and stables, through the floor boards of which rose heat from the animals below. Unfortunately the warmth was commonly dissipated by draughts through the roof, but at least there was hay and straw as bedding. Charles Waistell, an agriculturalist who wrote of such sleeping quarters in his *Designs for Agricultural Buildings, Labourers' Cottages and Farm Houses*, 1827, does not mention animal warmth, only smells and exhalations which he considered, like draughts, injurious to health.

It was shown by experiment a few years ago that actually pumping filtered air from a roomful of animals into an adjacent room will raise the temperature in that room. However the drawback of this calculated procedure is that in cold weather animals need all the heat they can produce while in hot weather their surplus heat is not wanted by human beings.

Chapter 5

Blazing Barns and Ricks

With the ending of the French wars there came, said the *Annual Register* for 1815, 'an extraordinary decline in agricultural prosperity'. Because of an extra good harvest in 1813 and plentiful supplies arriving from Ireland, the price of corn at last came down. Farmers' profits were reduced by half, but their rents, which had risen during the period of high war prices, stayed as they were. Difficult times for farmers continued for about twenty years, during which most farm buildings were not repaired or added to.

Farms were thrown up and, as notices to quit poured in, numbers of tenant farmers absconded. In 1815, according to Lord Ernle, thirty thousand acres of a small section of Huntingdonshire were abandoned and nineteen farms in the Isle of Ely became tenantless. Bankers pressed for their advances, landlords for their rents, tithe owners for their tithes and tradesmen for settlement of bills.

Everywhere farmers were dismissing men and the rural labour force, swelled by half a million returning soldiers and sailors, was either distressed or rebellious. The fall in prices was no comfort to them because wages, too, had fallen. A supplement to wages through the Poor Rate – this was anyway pegged to the price of bread – tended to demoralize the many who wanted to be independent.

From 1816 onwards sporadic outbreaks of rebellion disturbed the countryside and mobs of labourers demanded cheaper food and more pay. There were incidents in which they burned ricks and farm buildings, tore up enclosing fences, smashed threshing machines and insulted parish overseers by such actions as removing them from their houses on the parish dung cart.

Farmers were well advised in this period to keep some watch on their men. Charles Waistell wrote in *Designs for Agricultural Buildings* that in a farmhouse there 'should be at least one window on the ground floor belonging to a room that is constantly occupied, and the window of the farmer's bedroom should face the yard . . . stock and servants cannot be too much under the eye of their master.'

Troops were often called out and arrests became commonplace. The magistrates tried hard to be reasonable and to mediate, but as the years passed and unrest continued, well-to-do people living in the country began to have serious fears of a revolution on the lines of the recent French Revolution. Indeed, on 15 November 1830, a Paris newspaper carried the headline 'A Revolution in England'. The battlements that appeared on various Regency farm buildings – see the lime kiln illustrated in Part Two – reflected thoughts of defensive action as well as a fashion for the Gothic taste.

By November 1830 the anti-threshing machine riots in southern England looked dangerous and the judiciary became so harsh that labourers were being imprisoned and sent to Australia for sour looks and discontented conversation. Public meetings were forbidden. Although the rioting grew less flagrant, the crime of arson remained common – culprits could rarely be found. The incendiary fires of Kent distressed the artist Samuel Palmer when he was living at Shoreham (Geraldine Norman, *The Times*, 25 March 1981) and a rich mauve cloud of smoke floats about his landscape water-colour of about 1830 *Ightham Moat: the harvesters hurrying away the last of the harvest*. A Wiltshire farmer who reduced wages one Saturday from 10 shillings a week to 9 half-expected a visit from an angry mob waving sticks: instead he found on the Sunday that his farmstead was in flames.

In December 1830 farm buildings and hayricks were ablaze throughout England as far north as Carlisle, and at night families in easy circumstances trembled behind barred doors as farm labourers and others strode about shouting revolutionary slogans. A leader-writer for *The Times* observed on 6 December:

> Let the rich be taught that Providence will not suffer them to oppress their fellow creatures with impunity. Here are tens of thousands of Englishmen, industrious, kind-hearted, but broken-hearted beings, exasperated into madness by insufficient food and clothing, by utter want of necessaries for themselves and their unfortunate families.

Civil peace was achieved in 1831, but only after Lord Melbourne had given his approval for the taking of appalling measures. In one three-week period three demonstrators were hanged and 420 taken from their families (no provision was made for these) and transported to Australia as convicts. As the men marched chained together to the docks, they attracted, it was reported in the papers, much sympathy from the crowds.

Within months the insurrection gradually died down and life for the rural labourers resumed its accustomed course, though it was now bleaker than ever. If little has been made of these troubles in the history books it may be, as Mr Whitlock suggested in *The Times* of 21 November 1980, because the people most intimately concerned were not those who read or wrote history – and also because the riots failed. The true seriousness of the troubles which were at last so cruelly stamped on is apparent from a look at the newspapers of the time; a surprising circumstance which these reveal is that some of the arrested rioters were farmers or tradesmen.

As for why there was no French Revolution in England (one result in France was the transformation at a stroke of all rent-paying peasants into peasant-owners), the simplified answer must be that whereas in France the crushing servitude of the peasants was administered by paid officials called *intendants*, the almost powerless aristocracy being at Versailles, in England, on the other hand, the aristocracy and the rest of

Crank for a threshing machine to be operated by twelve men, 1831 (J. C. Loudon, *Encyclopaedia of Agriculture*)

the landowning class were present on their estates, supreme there and often powerful in the government.

By the mid-1830s farming was showing signs of recovery, but its buildings were more neglected-looking than they had been at the beginning of the century. Often sited at the extreme end of the holding – despite the enclosures – they generally consisted of large barns, a stable and yard for carthorses and a shed for carts. Cattle tended to be worse housed than the carts and had draughty, rickety sheds ranged round a soggy yard. There in winter they subsisted on starvation rations and looked emaciated after being driven to a distant market. Farm roads were few, and so usual was deep mud that sheep were bred for length of leg to enable them to be driven from place to place. Very little land was drained.

However, threshing machines had been available since the 1780s for farmers bold enough to cut down on labour in the interests of a faster and fuller yield from a given number of sheaves; the machines were much discussed in such journals as the *Farmer's Magazine* and the *Farmer's Journal* and, although not all farmers could read, agriculture was being conducted more efficiently than the appearance of the farm buildings would have suggested.

Sheep were popular on the farm, everyone now realizing that they survived well as outdoor animals and needed no buildings. However, farmers were made aware in 1839, by a report in the *Agricultural Magazine*, that sheep grew better, and fewer lambs died, when they were provided with winter shelter – not to raise the temperature of their surroundings, but just to protect them from wind, rain and snow.

John Childers, MP, had carried out a controlled experiment between January 1 and April 1. He had forty wethers and put twenty in a yard having access to a shed with a raised floor of rough boards which was just large enough for all of them to lie down at once. He put the other twenty in a field, a sandy field which was tolerably sheltered. Both lots were given the same amount of food: 27 stones of cut turnips each day between them, 10 lb linseed cakes, 10 pints of barley, an armful of hay and a constant supply of salt. At the beginning the two groups ate about the same amount, but before long the sheep with a shelter were eating a fifth less than the others. At the end of the three months they had gained weight calculated as being greater by a third than those in the open.

Other accounts of better progress made by winter-sheltered sheep followed. During the 1850s, in Somerset and elsewhere, wheeled sheds with slatted floors were moved about the fields on rails – to save undue treading of the soil – and J. C. Morton reported in *The Prince Consort's Farms*, 1863, that Prince Albert liked to house fattening sheep in a building with a slatted floor, and found that they 'throve fast compared with the progress made out of doors'. The drawback to such arrangements, convenient though they were at lambing time, was the extra work of so cleaning the shelters that the sheep remained in health, no animals being more likely than sheep to pass on disease when clustered together. Winter housing of sheep was therefore unusual in the nineteenth century, and it remains the exception today.

Meanwhile farmers hindered by bad buildings, and labourers by bad lodgings, had a kindly and indefatigable champion in John Claudius Loudon. A Scottish farmer's son, born in 1783, he made himself the only

Boring for water, 1831 (J. C. Loudon, *Encyclopaedia of Agriculture*)

designer of farm buildings to be given a place in the *Dictionary of National Biography*. Farmer, land agent, town planner, architect and travelled writer on gardens and trees, he was an enthusiast who could devote as much attention in his writings to the furnishings of a farm worker's cottage – taking in boot scrapers, knives, forks and pegs for wet clothes – as to the latest farmgate and steam-driven threshing machine. Nor was he scornful, as Cobbett was, of farmers indulging a taste for mahogany furniture, carpets and cut glass. He gave paternal advice on how to embellish the farmhouse.

Loudon's astonishing *Encyclopaedia of Agriculture*, with 1,375 pages of small print, appeared in 1831 and the even more astonishing – and better – *Encyclopaedia of Cottage, Farm and Villa Architecture*, with 670 of its 1,138 pages devoted to buildings and machines for farmers, appeared a mere two years later, thanks to Loudon's habit of taking no more than four hours' sleep a night. The latter book, especially, drew the interest of landowners, bailiffs and designers concerned with rural buildings; it did so at just the time when agriculture was showing signs of the recovery called for by there being in England and Wales nearly four million more mouths to feed than ten years previously.

Loudon believed that if farmers applied to their work the principles of manufacturing industry, there would be endless opportunities for them to prosper modestly. 'The main comfort of all those in agriculture will ever consist more in the *possession within themselves of the essential means of a comfortable existence* [his italics] than in the power of accumulating fortunes.' Despite his own unremitting labour, generally done while suffering from rheumatism which led eventually to the amputation of an arm, Loudon was ever concerned about the comfort of those working on the land.

Nineteenth-century farmwork tended to be uncomfortable, of course, for most of the year, and Loudon considered ways of reducing hardship by means of more sensible and better-sited buildings; he described them by the hundred (this one would do, that one was better), aware that farmers generally had little idea of what was being done in other parts of the country. He urged consideration for animals, too. Carters were to wash their horses' feet in the stable instead of riding them through a pond while hot from the plough or cart and thus put them at risk of catching cold. Where the lodging of bachelor labourers was amidst the farm buildings, their sleeping place should be connected with stable and cowhouse by speaking tubes 'in order that the men may more readily hear any noise made in the night-time'.

Loudon had plenty to say about the poor accommodation that was general for farm servants, those who were boarded neither in the farmer's nor the bailiff's house, and about the garrets and smelly storerooms in which female servants had to sleep.

The agricultural cottages of the time were deplorable. Loudon said so repeatedly. But what moved him to bitter sarcasm was the sort of apparently well-off landlord who let his designer erect brand-new cottages for married labourers which consisted of one room only. In the matter of cottages, Loudon was peculiarly influential, and as the century went on thousands of farm labourers owed their cottage garden to his insistence in both encyclopedias that a bit of ground must be provided for a married man to grow vegetables.

Chapter 6

Nineteenth-Century Architectural Style

The incorporation of architectural shapes and features in the designs published by J. C. Loudon may now seem irrelevant for workaday buildings of the farmstead. Many assume that form follows function and that only colour and outline have to be considered. In Loudon's time a person of substance with a new building on hand liked it to exhibit the trimmings of architecture and to be better than just traditional or functional.

It could be either gothic or classical: in the Battle of the Styles Loudon was neutral. And although, in deference to a reaction to the serene classicism of the eighteenth century, most of his cottages are gothic, most of his farm buildings are classical and either Grecian or Italianate. But popular taste, already influenced by him, was favouring a variety of more or less romantic styles from the past, including the indeterminate Old English, a superior version of the so-called vernacular. In the two encyclopedias referred to there was something for all preferences, and farm buildings in the manner of, say, Normandy were put in as readily as designs inspired by the Continental travel of an architect called Peter Robinson.

In his slim volume *Designs for Farm Buildings*, 1830, Robinson had sought to interest landowners in barns and cowsheds exhibiting a home-made Swiss or Italian style. He made no secret of doing what architects have often been accused of doing – merely adding decoration to an already serviceable structure. The best plans for farm buildings, Robinson considered, had already been established; but too many were dull and crude through being the work of the unassisted village carpenter. 'It is the external form that I consider may be improved, without affecting the plan . . . the mere shed may create a degree of interest by a proper arrangement of the materials with some regard to the outline.'

Although always concerned with utility, Loudon was happy on the whole for his readers to dress their farm buildings in whichever way they found pleasing to the eye – though he did make fun of English cattle having to rub themselves against the fake ruins of Grecian columns. .

He explained the effects that could be produced and wrote as follows, after giving directions for the erection of a farmer's brick-making kiln: 'The expression of local connection and character may be given by the form of arches or other prominent parts being adopted which follow those that are most striking in an adjoining bridge or other public building.'

To display style in farm buildings the main resource, he said, was the expression of the walls; and as these were usually only one storey high, it was chiefly affected by the supports of the roof. The form of the roof was a second source of style, and that of the openings and windows a third. But he put in a caution about going too far, and said that a display of the smaller ornaments peculiar to the different architectural styles was 'altogether unsuitable for buildings in use for carrying on the business of a farm'. His farmery in the Grecian style avoids this fault, as the

Barn in Italian style, 1830 (Peter Robinson, *Designs for Farm Buildings*)

illustration shows; it makes a useful complex, compact and symmetrical.

Neither the early Victorians nor the Georgians before them set much store by genuinely old buildings. One's house or farmstead should be new; modern was a very popular word. Loudon, versatile as always, was happy to be a preservationist. He recommended that Elizabethan and medieval houses, deserted and left to nature, should be turned into farm buildings. 'Under a higher degree of civilization, conversion takes the place of destruction and things merely change their owners or their uses.' He would not really wish fine specimens of architecture to be occupied as farmeries, 'yet we have thought it a duty to throw out this hint with a view at least of preventing them from being rashly pulled down'.

The upper floors of country houses, he said, 'should be used as wool-lofts and for storing bulky yet light articles; the next floor for poultry, rabbits or other small animals; the floor below for ewes and lambs, or swine; the first floor for cattle and horses; the ground floor for barns, cart-sheds, tool-houses, etc.; and the cellar floor for storing roots.' Where it was planned to use the upper floors as a manufactory and only the lower parts for agriculture, he considered that 'one large steam engine on the ground floor might suffice for both establishments.'

If all floors were to be used for agriculture, it was of course necessary to construct inclined planes to reach them, these being either outside or inside the building; and Loudon reminded readers that at some of the large hotels in London the horses were lodged on the first floor (horses

Barn in Swiss style, 1830 (Peter Robinson, *Designs for Farm Buildings*)

are so accommodated at a London military barracks today), the carriages being on the ground floor. Ascent and descent were by means of litter-strewn ramps at an angle of 25–30°.

But in country houses of a spacious kind, said Loudon, 'the inclined planes need not be so steep, and they ought not to be covered with litter, which is a clumsy contrivance – and in London at least, renders the air of stables of this description intolerable.' Where the disused house had only two storeys, conversion was easy: he referred to the manner in which it was commonly carried out in Poland. It is not known on what scale Loudon's suggestions were taken up, but at Rochford Hall, near Southend, there is certainly one good example to be seen of a house of Henry VIII's time which in the nineteenth century was made into a barn.

Converting farm buildings into better farm buildings became a recommended undertaking from the late 1830s, as increasingly it seemed sensible to change the fixed equipment of a farm to meet the requirements of a type of agriculture that was more industrial. At this time the demand for food was noticeably increasing. In a census – the first taken had been in 1801 – it emerged that the population England and Wales rose from 12 million in 1821 to 16 million in 1841.

It rose to 20 million in 1861 and to 26 million in 1881, and during most of the period there were enough good farmers to take advantage profitably of the opportunity to supply a growing market, and to do it without help, or competition from abroad. Thanks to this minority of effective farmers, the result was an economic achievement and 'the development', in the words of Nigel Harvey, 'of a farming system which raised the art and science of food production to a pitch never before seen, so that visitors from the Old and New World alike marvelled at the efficiency, the prosperity and the professional pride of the British agricultural industry.'

Along with works of adaptation, entirely new farmsteads were being put up from the late 1830s. These tended to serve three kinds of farm: (1) the holding on land just reclaimed from the remaining areas of waste land; (2) the holding created by belated enclosure of open fields or common grazings; and (3) the holding created by enclosure in the eighteenth century or earlier but still operated from a village farmhouse – many such houses had now been divided into cottages for farm labourers.

The Victorian farmstead, described by an editor of the *Farmer's Magazine* as one great stationary machine, was the means by which heavier crops were prepared for the market or converted by extra numbers of animals into meat, milk, butter, cheese and, crucially, manure. The best farmsteads of these high farming times were not radically different from their Georgian predecessors, just improved versions of them.

But any overall improvement depended on the landlords. The bigger ones had agents and other professional advisers to see about new farm buildings and to guide tenant farmers on how to keep them in repair. But those who were willing to have this work carried out were not typical. Nor was the conscientious smaller landlord of the sort picked out by Richard Jefferies for an essay in the 1870s called 'An Ambitious Squire': this describes how a young man, on coming into an estate of modest size, contrived to improve it for the benefit of his tenants and himself.

After he had had the place for a little while, there was not a square inch of waste ground to be found. When the tenants were callous to hints, the squire gave them pretty clearly to understand that he meant his land to be improved. . . . He himself of his own free motive and initiative ordered new buildings to be erected where he, by personal inspection, saw that they would pay. . . . There was a distinct increase in the revenue of the estate after the first two years. The increase arose in part from the diminished expenses, for it had

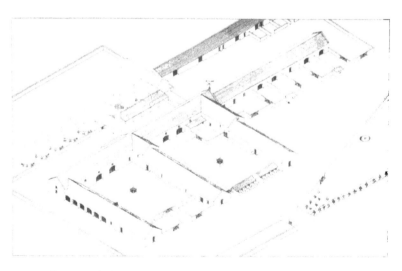

Farmstead, 1844 (Henry Stephens,
The Book of the Farm)

been found that a tumbledown place is more costly to maintain than one in good repair. The tenants at first were rather alarmed, fearing lest the change should end in a general rise of rents. It did not. By degrees he acquired a reputation as the most just of landlords. His tenantry were not only satisfied, but proud of him. Yet all these things had been done for his own interest – so true is it that the interest of the landlord and the tenant are identical.

Sir James Caird, in a report called *English Agriculture in 1850–1*, wrote of well-designed farmsteads that were the rural equivalent of the factories which were making England the workshop of the world; he also pointed to the majority of farm buildings as evidence of low standards of estate management. Nigel Harvey draws special notice to the following passage from Caird:

The inconvenient, ill-arranged hovels meant a cow shelter, the rickety wood and thatched barns and sheds devoid of any known improvement for economising labour, food and manure, which are to be met with in every county in England, and from which anything else is exceptional in the southern counties, are a reproach to the landlords in the eyes of all skilful agriculturalists who see them. One can hardly believe that such a state of affairs is permitted in an old and wealthy country.

Barn and cattle sheds in Old English style, 1830 (Peter Robinson, *Designs for Farm Buildings*)

In the same year a similar comment was made by J. Ewart in his *Treatise on the Arrangement of Agricultural Buildings*, 1851:

> How frequently in all parts of the United Kingdom are the various offices arranged in relative positions ill suited to the intended purposes and without any appearance of design – dropped, as it were by mere chance, into the places they occupy.

But whatever the farm buildings looked like in the 1850s (twenty years later Caird reported a general improvement), the work in and around them progressed much better than anyone had expected. Despite setbacks caused by diseases in crops and animals, English agriculture prospered between 1840 and 1875 in a way which was envied by other countries of Europe. In the earlier part of this period the zest of the keen farmers was made noticeable to travellers by the glaring contrasts between good and bad farmsteads.

One innovation in the farmstead which always attracted attention was the tall chimney called for by the employment of a steam engine. Many barns had already been adapted for a threshing machine and had a neat round wheelhouse attached, in which horses circled to drive the threshing machine. Now came adaptation for steam and advice from Loudon on how to achieve chimneys as elegant as the factory-stacks of Glasgow.

Several firms competed in the manufacture of steam-driven barn

Barn and threshing-floor, 1845 (*Mansell Collection*)

machinery, which threshed the corn, raised the straw to where it was wanted, winnowed and dressed the grain and poured it into sacks ready for the market. The stationary steam engine helped, too, in the livestock departments: it was made to pump water, grind corn, crush cattle cake, split beans, cut chaff, pulp turnips and boil pig food. Theoretically nearly as much mechanical aid was available for the farmer as at the beginning of the twentieth century. John Morton could write proudly in *The Prince Consort's Farms*, 1863, '. . . in the past 20 years the agricultural-ist has benefited by scientific research, by mechanical ingenuity and by increasing skill more than during any period in our history.'

In the 1860s new buildings on farms began to look different. The growth of industry and the coming of a railway network made it no longer necessary for rural builders to depend on local materials; and tiles, slates and machine-made bricks were being conveyed to all parts – not just to those having a waterway – and replacing earth, timber and thatch. Often even local supplies of stone were ignored in favour of cheap brick.

Loudon, who wrote his encyclopedias in the 1830s when building materials were obtained on the spot as a matter of course, had seen the change coming. J. B. Denton, publishing *The Farm Homesteads of Eng-land* in 1863, saw it arrive, and, in the course of discussing in a practical manner the siting, planning and erection of farm buildings, he recom-mended few materials that were procurable locally; but he did remark that bought materials were not necessarily superior to the home-produced which 'should not be hastily set aside'.

Corrugated iron for roofs and concrete made with Portland cement for foundations were both introduced in the 1860s, and for fitting up farm buildings it was now possible to buy cast iron partitions for stalls, cast iron pig troughs, iron rails and rollers for sliding doors, and trucks on rails for taking sheaves to the threshing machine and fodder to the troughs.

Farmers who acquired strong modern buildings at this time had a good investment for future generations if not for themselves: no one could have foreseen how long they were to last. The time for the average landowner or independent farmer to undertake agricultural building was to come to an end within a decade or so.

Chapter 7

A Use for Old Rolling Stock

In the late 1870s England was a powerful manufacturing nation; markets were expanding and industrial profits comparatively easy to gain. But for England's farmers everything was beginning to go wrong.

Free trade now ruled and overseas growers were producing wheat on virgin prairies, reaping it with mechanical reapers and sending it by rail and steamship to Britain: instead of being allies in the work of feeding a fast-expanding population, the North American farmers had become alarming competitors. The result of the flood of cheap corn was that British corn selling at 55 shillings a quarter in the mid-1870s fetched only 22 shillings in the 1890s. Corn was not the only worry: meat, butter and cheese from Australia, New Zealand, the United States and Denmark undersold the British farmer and set the price he could get. No longer did prices go up when bad weather caused a shortfall; the depression was worst in the corn-growing east where rainfall is lower than in the wetter grass regions of the west.

The government was unwilling and largely unable to help, while the railway companies actually hindered by quoting preferential rates for the carriage of imported supplies. Foreign countries were paying for English manufactured goods with cheap food. Even home-produced cheese, which yielded farmers no profit at less than fourpence a pound wholesale, was matched on occasion by Canadian cheese that was being sold at twopence a pound retail.

The average farmer did not own his holding, so he had no building on which to recoup if his farm finally collapsed under pressure from creditors. 'No man drinks the bitter cup of poverty to the dregs like the declining farmer,' wrote Richard Jefferies in an essay of 1879.

> The descent is so slow; there is time to drain every drop. It may take eight, or ten or 15 years. He cannot, like the bankrupt tradesman,

even when the fatal notice comes, put up his shutters and at once retire from view. Even at the end, after the notice, six months at least must elapse before all is over – before the farm is surrendered, and the sale of household furniture and effects takes place. He is in full public view all that time. So far as his neighbours are concerned he is in public view for years previously. He has to rise in the morning and meet them in the fields. He sees them in the road; as he goes by they look after him, and perhaps audibly wonder how long he will last.

People were less kind in those money-conscious and class-conscious Victorian times, and the wife of the failing farmer was allowed to suffer, too. Jefferies wrote:

She was conspicuously omitted from the social gatherings that occur from time to time. The neighbours' wives do not call; their well-dressed daughters, as they rattle by to the town in basket-carriage or dog-cart, look askance at the shabby figure walking slowly on the path beside the road. They criticise the shabby shawl; they sneer at the slow step which is the inevitable result of hard work, the cares of maternity and of age.

In telling the story of a particular farmer, Jefferies observed:

All this blind work of his was of no avail against the ocean steamer and her cargo of wheat and meat from the teeming regions of the West. Nor was it of avail against the fall of prices and the decreased yield consequent upon a succession of bad seasons.

But in the pages of *Francis Kilvert's Journal*, 1870–1879, the slow decay of British agriculture seems barely perceptible; in a remote part of Herefordshire on the Welsh border there was not much from the outside world to affect the life of a country clergyman.

Years went by with nothing getting generally better, only slightly worse. At the end of the century a typical local paper comment, as quoted by Michael Winstanley in *Life in Kent*, 1978, ran as follows:

Unfavourable seasons, now unrelieved by any advance in prices, have exhausted the capital of tenant farmers and many of them cannot choose but go. Lucky those men who ten or fifteen years ago retired from agricultural pursuits while there was yet a balance at the bank. – *Kentish Gazette*, October 1895.

A steam threshing contractor, recalling those days, told Mr Winstanley in the 1970s: 'You were a lucky man if you could make a farmer smile, especially when pay time came. I've had them cry. I've had them swear . . . the pub was their place and that's where the money went, I suppose.' On the part of the general public there was indifference, if not contempt, for the problems of those who tilled the land, and intelligent boys who went as pupils to farmers tended to leave for a town job because of jeers from contemporaries.

The effect on farm buildings was that less and less was done to them and hardly any new ones were built. The farming publications offered advice on how to prolong the life of existing buildings with the least expense. W. J. Malden in *Farm Buildings*, 1896, drew farmers' attention to the total loss through fire that could result from having all buildings

A Welsh pigsty, 1845 (*Mansell Collection*)

together in a tight group; most of the experts reminded farmers about covered cattle yards for the sake not of the cattle but of the manure, the valuable residues of which could be washed away by rain. One landlord-farmer who took up the idea rather late, perhaps because he lived in low-rainfall East Anglia – was H. Rider Haggard, who said in a January diary entry for 1899:

> To-day I have been making a plan for roofing in the horse and cattle yard at Bedingham with galvanised iron supported by oak posts. If it is possible, I am anxious to deal thus with all my open yards, as I believe that the expense of closing them in, which, if one can provide the necessary timber, is not so very great, will be repaid in three years by the manure saved and the increase of its fertilising value. I have already three such sheds erected over yards and there is no comparison between the stuff that comes from beneath them and that from the open pen which is frequently little better than dirty, rain-washed straw.

In the final decade of the nineteenth-century farms were often hard to let, despite a reduced rent and efforts by landlords to pull the buildings together. Yet not many years earlier land had been valuable for what it would yield and there was no question of tenant farmers declining or throwing up a holding because of defective buildings. The position now was that just when the owner of the soil could least afford it, he had to try to make up for the neglect of his predecessors. But cosmetic treatment rarely helped to let a farm: Malden noted in 1896 that 'in almost all parts of the country there are large blocks of buildings standing idle on unlet farms'.

Soon it became common for landlords to sell off sections of their estates at modest prices and there was thus created a new class of hopeful owner-occupiers of small farms. By 1914 these owner-occupiers were to own 10 per cent of the agricultural land of England and by 1939, 30 per cent. Without members of the landed gentry to supervise, at least in theory, the design and appearance of the farm buildings, the reign of economy became increasingly obvious. It was around 1900 that decayed railway sleepers first came to be used for the walls of sheds and yards. Corrugated iron, invented back in the 1860s, was now in common use, often for unsightly patches. Before long old railway carriages, old goods vans and redundant Nissen huts became common objects around the farms, and in course of time they seemed part of the rural tradition.

The frustrations of agricultural life led to a great consumption of beer, and if there was one type of farm building which remained trim and carefully repaired it was the oasthouse of south-east England in which the hop flowers were dried. New oasthouses – of the kind now traditional with cowl-topped kilns – were being built throughout the nineteenth century and into the twentieth.

Untold gallons of beer were consumed by gloomy farmers in rough pubs and by workers in the fields. Richard Jefferies wrote in 1880:

> The limit of the labourer's liquor power has never yet been reached. A man will lie on his back in the harvest field, under a hedge sweet with the June roses that smile upon the hay, and never move or take his lips away till a gallon has entered his being, for it can hardly be said to be swallowed. Two gallons a day is a not uncommon consumption with men who swing the scythe or reaping hook.

Hops, it came to be realized, could be grown intensively and prove year after year a rewarding crop. The expanding and powerful breweries could never get enough: Bass, Ratcliff and Gretton of Burton-on-Trent were so rich that in the 1880s and 1890s they could send a party of 10,000 employees and their families for an expensive annual outing by train.

Apart from their essential drying function, the oasts served as social centres during the September hopping season. For large numbers of working people hop-picking remained until the early 1950s the one holiday in the year. They came to Kent in hordes from London, and also from villages throughout the south. In *Country Calendar*, Flora Thompson said that 'exhilarating excitement attended the setting off of the contingent' from her village in Hampshire. It consisted mainly of women and children and one or two unemployed men and boys; they went hopping every year as much for pleasure as for profit. 'Mothers who have a sickly or ailing child make a special point of going, for the scent of the hops has a reputation as a cure for all ills.'

Chapter 8

Cowhouse Economy

A readiness to change course characterized those farmers who survived the depression. Some did well by switching largely to poultry or, if they were near towns, to market gardening. The cheapness of the imported corn they complained about encouraged keeping livestock, and even the penurious labourers in Flora Thompson's *Lark Rise* could afford a little barley meal to help fatten their pig. The labourer's sty, attached to his cottage, was of the pen-and-run type which remained almost universal until the 1930s. A farmer with a busy dairy would have a row of them. Richard Jefferies, describing in *Toilers of the Field* a typical farmhouse dairy in the 1890s, related that the buttermilk and refuse ran by a channel across the court into a vault sunk in the ground, from which it was dipped for the pigs. The vault was closed by a heavy wooden lid.

Sheep could be profitable and had the advantage of making no demands on the farmstead, but of all the farming enterprises taken up in the depression the keeping of dairy cattle was the most likely to succeed, especially if undertaken within reach of a large farm. Liquid milk, unlike cheese, was one of the few foods which could not be imported; so contracts with the big milk retailers were competed for and between 1880 and 1930 the cow population of England and Wales rose from nearly two million to nearly four million. The cowhouse or byre in which the cows were milked by hand became the most important building on the farm, though no one would have supposed this from looking at the average specimen. Only here and there was money expended on building brick cowhouses to meet textbook specifications to do with ventilation, lighting, feeding places and disposal of dung. Such buildings made news and got photographed. The average farmer just crowded his cows into the buildings he had, tying them up in pairs.

Textbooks reflect the urge to economize and the 1908 edition of

Stephens's *Book of the Farm* told farmers obliged to erect a new cowhouse that its roof could perfectly well 'consist of trees covered with broom, whin, fern or branches of spruce'. It paid better to accept limitations than to rebuild; and the dairy farmer just worked away to fill his churns and get them off by horse and cart to the nearest railway station.

Housewives or their cooks readily bought it by the scoopful from churns brought by horse float to their doors, no one thinking much about the conditions under which the milk might have been produced. The authorities thought about this, however, and were well aware that much of the milk the doctors recommended for building a healthier nation was capable of causing harm.

Since an Act of Parliament of 1885, the local councils had been framing by-laws about making the interiors of cowhouses easy to clean and reasonably hygienic, but the regulations proved virtually unenforceable. And so slow were the inspectors of the district councils in making even an impact that Rider Haggard, novelist-turned-landlord and active farmer, was able to write in 1899: 'I believe there exist inspectors of dairies, though I never saw or heard of one inspecting my dairy, and I doubt whether the duty is half so efficiently or strictly performed as it ought to be.' He had been reading in the papers of tuberculosis in cows and of the tuberculin test and observed:

It was only in the past year or so that I first heard of one or the other. But science is always revealing fresh horrors for our sight, and I have little doubt that the experts speak the truth when they say that a great deal of consumption is caused by tuberculous milk. For aught I know, one consumes it daily in one's tea.

It was useless, said Rider Haggard, to expect one farmer in twenty to bother his head about the matter. 'I know that when I took over this farm, I found that into the pond from which the cows drank was led the entire sewage of a yard. I dare say that any inspector who took an interest in his work could make even worse discoveries.' (Shortly after this entry, an inspector did call on Rider Haggard, finding various faults.)

Eventually the Milk and Dairies Order of 1926, backed up by the appointment of more and better trained inspectors, at last brought it home to some farmers that dirty milking sheds and milkers with dirty hands often led to a culpable distribution of infected milk; that milk when warm was a magnificent breeding ground for a number of bacteria, most of these just spoiling the milk but others being harmful to those who drank it; that a cowhouse ought at least to have a concrete floor with suitable slopes and be regularly swilled out – to drains whose gratings were outside and not inside the building.

G. T. Garratt, a Cambridgeshire farmer, wrote critically of his own cowsheds in *Hundred Acre Farm*, 1928. Wondering how it was possible that they had passed an inspection under the Dairies Order, he reflected that 'literally enforced, the Order would stop all milk production on most of our mixed farms'. Production of milk for sale was in fact stopped on the small farm in Suffolk which Adrian Bell worked in the 1920s. In his autobiographical novel *The Cherry Tree* he amusingly described being interrupted to show an inspector where he milked his one cow: this was either in a 'rough shelter of thatch and upended faggots or in a strawed partition in a barn'.

At this time, as Garratt wrote and others have recalled since, the bulk of the nation's milk was not graded to a standard; it was just sold as whole milk for domestic use, the same liquid going for the making of cheese and milk chocolate. Controls to do with tuberculosis were largely ineffective.

The only two grades of milk known to the public were Grade A and Grade A Tuberculin Tested. The first was in fact the lowest grade of all and did not ensure a higher standard of hygiene than that under which the most ordinary milk was produced. The second grade was confused with the first and the public thought they were getting it from tested cows. While the retailers freely fixed winter and summer prices, the farmer's only business was to produce as much milk as he could of a quality that would escape trouble from the police.

In Garratt's experience, the London firms seldom worried so long as cowhouses reached early Victorian standards of cleanliness and the milk did not go sour. He could not help admiring, he wrote, the effrontery with which they carried out their end of the business. He once saw a van in London belonging to the firm to which he sent his milk and on it there was this advertisement: 'Special Milk for Invalids from our Own Farms'.

The first practicable milking machine, enabling more than one cow to be milked at the same time, had appeared after decades of experiment in the early 1900s. But acceptance was extremely slow and cautious, the farmers saying they preferred hand milking and the milkmaids fearing the loss of their jobs; in 1939 it was reckoned that only 8 per cent of herds (15 per cent of all cows) were milked mechanically. However, the vacuum pump, teat cups and pipes did no more in those days than transfer milk from udders to bucket to cooler to churn; under present-day arrangements it is taken by overhead pipes to huge cooling vessels. Churns stood at farm gates awaiting collection by the retailer's lorry.

Through adjustment to changed circumstances and systematic development, milk production went up enormously between the wars, and vast businesses grew up in Cheshire and Lancashire to supply the industrial conurbations. Not everyone, though, was a customer. Surveys showed that about a quarter of the people living in 'poor working class districts' drank no milk at all; but the figures overall, as issued by the Ministry of Agriculture, suggest the impressive increase in output: an estimated 864 million gallons in 1913 rose to 1,425 million gallons in 1934, a quantity which was in fact too much by over 100 million gallons for the population to consume. According to a report by the Milk Reorganisation Commission in 1933 – quoted by Tom Williams in *Labour's Way to Use the Land* – the consumption in the towns of England was about 15 gallons a head a year. The comparable figure was much higher elsewhere: in the United States, 48 gallons; in Denmark, 57 gallons; in Switzerland, 83 gallons.

Although it was poverty – three million people were unemployed in 1933 – rather than misgivings about quality which accounted for England's comparatively low consumption, the potential danger of drinking milk had become a matter of grave embarrassment to the health authorities by the early 1930s, for bovine tuberculosis was now reckoned to kill over 2,500 people a year and to cause a greater number of illnesses. 'The incidence of bovine tuberculosis is probably as high in Britain as anywhere in the world,' said an Economic Advisory Commission report in May 1934. 'At least 40 per cent of the cows are infected.' In the United States, where cowhouses were extensive models of cleanliness, only 1.6 per cent of the cows were infected.

In May 1935, at a meeting of a rural district council in the Midlands, the sanitary inspector reported that, out of 94 cowhouses just inspected, 24 were incapable of improvement and ought to be pulled down (*Farm Economist*, January 1936). During and just after the Second World War farmers were strenuously encouraged by means of grants to acquire proper buildings and equipment for milk production, and teams of milk-sampling officers were sent out by the district councils to check the safety of milk before it left the farms.

An urban cowhouse still functioning in the City of London in 1952 was no more than an amusing survival, but even at that date, as I learn from Jack Stringer, former milk inspector for a Hertfordshire council, it was usual to find great contrasts in the standard of hygiene on cow-keeping

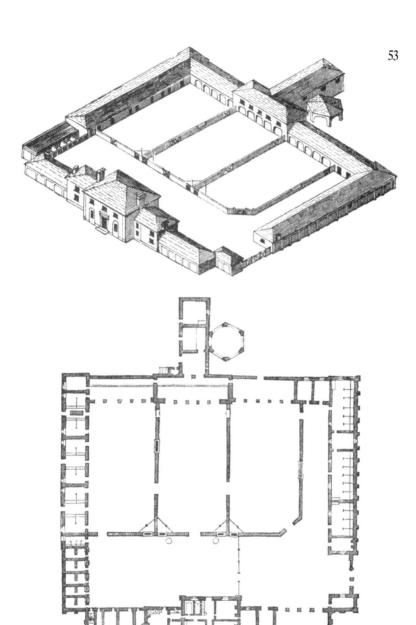

Farmstead with Italian influence. Note wheelhouse.
Farmhouse contains a parlour, kitchen, business room, living
room, pantry, dairy, store room and brewhouse, 1827 (Charles
Waistell, *Designs for Agricultural Buildings*)

farms. At one, the cowhouse and attendant dairy would have the hospital-like sterility of glazed brick and stainless steel; at another, rotten wooden walls would shelter pails of milk whose whiteness barely concealed the manure which had fallen in during the hand-milking. 'Even now', Stringer says, 'I have to brace myself if tempted to drink a glass of cold milk.'

Chapter 9

Seventy Years of Neglect

In its early twentieth-century, Edwardian phase, the long depression threw up the cases of hardship less dramatically. The weaker farmers had given up; thousands had emigrated – as had tens of thousands of labourers – and an attitude of resignation sustained those who continued or started farming. At least a farmer, so long as he remained on his holding, had no need to let his family go short of food.

Then came the First World War and at last a clamouring market for home-produced foodstuff which for a few years brought great financial rewards to the farmers. Many were tempted, mindful of the repeal of the Corn Production Act, to take more from their fields in crops than they put back in manure. Indeed, so infertile did much of the land become that it was said later that prosperity left the farmers poor in everything except money. In 1920 state-engineered protection ceased and once more the farmers had to compete with imports of cheap food. The one consolation was that they themselves could take advantage of cheap grain for fattening livestock. There was an uproar of agricultural complaint when in the early 1930s massive ordering from abroad made meat so cheap that some families were able for the first time to buy a little bacon.

Land gradually ceased to be cultivated (in 1933 two million fewer acres were farmed than in 1913) and landlords took to deserting the country for the city. A breaking-up of large estates led to an increase in the number of hopeful owner-occupiers of farms, young men who very often had felt compelled to buy. But, weighed down with mortgage payments and other burdens, few of these could take proper advantage of their freedom. There was no money to buy capital equipment, to experiment, to bring about changes. Indeed, lack of working capital made good farming almost impossible in the inter-war period and bankruptcies, as referred to in Adrian Bell's books about rural Suffolk, ceased to be news. A series of Wheat Acts, starting in 1931, were supposed to subsidize with guaranteed prices, but the scheme worked fitfully.

As for the farmsteads, the effect by the 1930s of sixty or seventy years of neglect was to give these buildings, which had once served an advanced system of agriculture, a markedly tumbledown appearance. Nigel Harvey has written the classic description of their slow decline.

> Gradually, tirelessly, the rain seeped through roofs of decaying thatch or slipping slates, through holes where the wind had torn away tiles that were not replaced, and rotted the supporting timbers. Water from choked or falling guttering crumbled away walls and undermined foundations. Unpainted woodwork failed to hold window panes or door hinges. There was no end to it. Year by year, the patient processes of decay and disintegration probed for weaknesses in the unmaintained buildings. Year by year they found less resistance and the slow, pervading degeneration they wrought became more obvious, less redeemable (*History of Farm Buildings*).

Innovatory structures for farmers were nevertheless being pressed on their attention in this period.

There were new silos for turning greenstuff into compressed cattle food, fully prefabricated Dutch barns for sheltering hay and fodder, and installations for drying the grain produced in a great mountain by combine harvesters. Engines and all kinds of processing machines had been much improved. For work out in the fields, the combines mentioned, reaping and threshing in one mobile operation, had been available since 1928. However, by 1939 England and Wales had between them only 150.

Silage-making, a crude form of canning, had been demonstrated by the Duke of Bedford on his estate in the 1880s, but most farmers still found it a troublesome procedure liable to mishaps, and some wooden silos erected in Norfolk soon went out of commission. The Dutch barn was the first farm building to which prefabrication – instead of making-up on the farm – was successfully applied.

The general agricultural textbooks and official publications of the 1930s offered what amounted to a preview of the future – in which stock would be farmed intensively (especially pigs and poultry), the farmstead thoroughly mechanized and equipped with milking parlours and foolproof installations for drying grain. But as the Cotswold farmer George Henderson has written: 'Very few farmers at that time used the resources of science which were at their disposal.'

Among these few was certainly Henderson himself. In his book *The Farming Ladder*, 1964, he described how he and his brother – self-taught, launched with a bank loan, doing their own building – contrived to make a steadily increasing profit throughout the 1920s and 1930s on a thin-soiled farm of 85 acres. Apart from devoting themselves to the farm to the exclusion of all other matters, and putting in 80 hours a week, the main reason for their success, which eventually drew conducted parties, was extra-heavy stocking. Sometimes cattle were tethered to make the most of odd corners. Every bit of manure, including liquid manure in tanks, was treated with care and spread over the land – even drainings from the silo were caught and re-used for making more silage. The rotation followed was fallow, corn, corn, one year of ley, corn.

Crops of corn, said Henderson, were at least good enough to clear expenses and, cashed through stock – that is, fed to animals – they would show a reasonable profit. 'When wheat dropped to 18 shillings a quarter, or a third of the cost of production, we could still keep our land under the plough by converting the grain into fattened poultry. You could see twopence-halfpenny worth of wheat, in a different form, for a shilling.' In 1942 he could announce: 'Twenty years of farming have enabled us to increase our output thirteen times and our capital a hundredfold.'

Henderson criticized the majority of farmers for trying to remedy the situation in which they found themselves by growing a bigger and bigger acreage of corn, with an invariably smaller and smaller yield, to be sold at lower and lower prices until they were as insolvent as their land was impoverished. The common solution of 'letting arable tumble down to grass' and farming with the proverbial sheepdog and roll of netting was also, he said, doomed to failure because profit depended on intensity of production, and more stock could in fact be carried on arable land.

Faced by so much makeshift farming, the professional designers of farm buildings were inactive, and in the whole period 1880 to 1939 only a handful of building textbooks appeared. Three of the authors contrived to choose the same title, *Modern Farm Buildings*. Unlike the Victorian farmers who turned to books for new ideas or design, the farmers of the 1930s were not keen to read advice on adapting their buildings, prefer-ring to read advertisements for cement and corrugated iron. Both these materials were a gift for immediate repairs and patching, and became increasingly noticeable about the farmsteads. Designing something new was a luxury, and farmers deciding, perhaps in a hurry, to go in for pigs, might not bother even with conventional piggeries. A survey of these, quoted by Nigel Harvey, revealed that a common use for the old railway rolling stock was for farrowing pigs, and that loose boxes and tool sheds were often used for fattening them; the pigs of the past, unlike today's, had a thick layer of fat over their backs to help keep them warm.

There can never have been a larger number of crumbling farm buildings than in 1939, the year in which the Second World War broke out. Some, of course, were no longer working buildings, but the rest continued to fulfil their allotted functions of storage, processing and animal sheltering. In 1939 Lord Addison, a minister of agriculture, wrote that it was difficult to 'exaggerate their dilapidation or the handicap it constitutes to good husbandry'.

But although the farm buildings were at their worst agriculturally, they were something else to a new race of urban motorists who had taken to exploring the country during summer weekends. To them the English countryside proved to be all they had dreamed of, ageless, tranquil, unchanging, a place straight from the story books; the picturesque buildings nestling in tumbled grass, or behind tall hedges, encouraged rambling clubs and painters of landscape; and they were an attraction for the many who in those days collected butterflies, beetles and birds' eggs.

Literate country lovers wrote books about country matters and the age-old ways of farmers; several would be ready for sale at Christmas. Even the swarms of flies appearing in a cowshed at milking time and the state of an elderly milker's hat were viewed as part of a charming scene.

It can be said with hindsight that for serious students of farming history, the year 1939 would have been the best of all years for observing a maximum number of untouched old buildings. They had at their disposal, in a countryside now more green than brown, a great strung-out museum of agricultural archeology, nearly every building bearing without accretion the imprint of former routines. Best of all, it was not really a museum. Amidst a largely late-Victorian setting, there were people earning their bread, real people in gaiters and waistcoats who touched their caps.

The Second World War, like the First, brought an end to the worry and pressure of foreign competition, replacing it with what the farmers always wanted, an urgent demand for home-produced food. Wartime farmers were still on their own financially, but the government was active with moral support; it usefully rationed livestock food and instituted war agricultural committees to advise, encourage and or-ganize.

'Make silage, make sure' was one of the slogans of those days and many farmers who took to silage in the war never gave it up. George Henderson's concrete silo cost him £75 in the early 1940s and saved him, he said, a £100 bill for cowcake in the first winter – assuming that somewhere he had been able to find any cowcake.

By the end of the war production was about 60 per cent higher than at the beginning. It is astonishing, looking back, to consider how so much was achieved with buildings which overall were by no means more reassuring in appearance than they had been pre-war. Very few farms had modernized cowhouses or properly constructed sheds for fattening beef. According to a survey carried out between 1941 and 1943, the buildings of no more than 39 per cent of English and Welsh farms could be classed as satisfactory.

The Agriculture Act of 1947 has been the foundation stone of agricultural policy since the war, though the form of support for prices changed when Britain joined the European Common Market in 1973. 'For the first time in history,' said Tom Williams, Minister for Agriculture announcing the 1947 Bill, 'the farmers will be able to plan ahead with certain knowledge of market and price.' Deficiency payments guaranteed farmers minimum prices for their main products, and at the same time food imports were subjected to tariffs and quotas (Marion Shoard, *The Theft of the Countryside*, 1981).

Good brains – scientific, technical and business – occupied themselves with ways of farming more intensively and much information was circulated on such matters as doing more jobs by powered machinery and the productive effect of artificial light and heat on livestock. The number of research publications multiplied amazingly after the war. By 1950 they were coming out at the rate of 180 a year and by 1960 at the rate of 400 a year. There was a proportionately greater flow of general and trade literature. Since no farmer could be expected to read very much of all this, a growing army of Ministry officials and commercial advisers came into being to cull the best points and pass them on; but even these people found it hard, as Nigel Harvey has said, to keep themselves informed.

Chapter 10

The Redundant Barn

Thousands of farms have been amalgamated since the 1950s and more barns than ever have become spare buildings. Redundant is the word generally used. Strangely enough, redundancy among barns was a topic of conversation a hundred and fifty years ago when mechanized threshing removed the need for storing an entire crop for flailing throughout the winter.

Arthur Young reported to the Board of Agriculture in 1810 that the barns of Suffolk were in general 'uselessly large' and Loudon wrote in 1833: 'On no description of farm buildings has so much needless expense been incurred as on barns.'

Many of the large corn barns of those times were already ancient, yet probably at least half are standing today. They survived because successions of farmers found the barn still had some uses and it was less trouble to keep it than clear it away; and because it was the handsomest building on the farm – if not, in timber-building areas, the strongest. In England alone, it can be guessed, there remain some 20,000 pre-Victorian untransformed barns.

Thanks ironically to technical advance, there is now a bigger variety of agricultural uses for barns than in 1830s and 1840s. Apart from storage of hay and straw – for which the Dutch barn gives easier access – today's farmer has to cope with the product of the combine harvester, a sudden mountain of grain needing weather-proof shelter. Grain-drying installations need shelter, too, and the combine harvester itself has to be parked during its eleven months of inactivity.

Here, of course, a difficulty arises. An entrance designed for the biggest hay waggon is too small for a combine, and drastic alteration spoils the proportions of the building, and can be almost impossible. What numerous farmers have done is to knock out one of the blank end walls. By that means the barn remains unchanged on three sides while the fourth, opened-up, side can be inconspicuous when its new wooden doors are shut.

As objects in the landscape old barns are much appreciated land-marks, even for drivers on a motorway, and it is unfortunate that thousands have disappeared since the 1950s; it is scant comfort that a few have reappeared as residences in New England, USA. The Farm Capital Grants Scheme of 1957 did not help. The emphasis of its production-conscious authors lay on building afresh and hardly at all on mending and adapting existing structures.

Allowed a water-tight roof, timber-framed and stone-built barns have shown that they can last for centuries without attention; but roofing work can be an expensive luxury to the owner-occupier or landlord if he is uncertain about the usefulness of the building. 'We are not in business', as I heard a farmer say, 'to keep old buildings beautiful for other people to look at.' To be maintained as a self-respecting part of the national heritage barns need a gainful purpose, as conservationists realized in the middle of the nineteenth century. Then, as now, unusual functions were discussed, and as a result several barns became churches.

In 1849 the *Agricultural Journal* printed a letter from Thomas Acland of Chippenham about arranging a large barn as a lodging house for farm boys. Acland had divided one end into three compartments which included a six-bed dormitory and a dining hall with the threshing floor as its dais. 'Five or seven lads', he wrote, 'have been housed and fed here throughout the past four years.... Several have become excellent ploughmen and won prizes. After work they occasionally amuse them-selves with cricket or other games, or with reading, writing and playing the flute.'

The description suggests, for that period, a perfectly good rural use for a barn. Many would momentarily pause, however, to read of the great doorways being bricked up and fitted with casement windows – but then the reflection comes that at least the possibility was left for a de-conversion job later on. Conversion to dwelling houses has long been the commonest fate for empty barns, and is better than demolition; but it remains the least visually welcome if only because of the windows put in. Barns have no windows, only ventilation slits. Nor do they have front doors, domestic chimneys, television aerials and rose gardens. Once equipped with these things, let alone drawing rooms, they cease to retain the character of a barn.

Desultory human habitation of a sort involving no outward change can be a different matter, and a proposal of 1980 for the stone-built field barns of the Peak District seemed excellent. It was proposed, with the backing of the Duchess of Devonshire and the Derbyshire Historic Buildings Trust, that the tenant hill farmers, few of whom prosper, should add a little to their income by letting out their disused field barns to hikers as overnight resting places. For the benefit of farmers wishing to do this on an official basis how many farmers, not on a main tourist track, would unofficially refuse a traveller leave to lay out a sleeping bag under cover?) it was suggested widely that the local authority should issue not planning permission – with attendant regulations about water, and wash basins for each sex – but an annual licence. At the time of writing, this alternative is gaining supporters.

Numerous other possible uses have been put forward, notably by Essex County Council. Their booklet of 1979, *Historic Barns. A Planning Appraisal*, stimulated several new thoughts on how to check the general disappearance of old barns. The authors were P. M. Richards and the authority on early house carpentry, C. A. Hewett – who did the drawings. The booklet argues among much else the merits, according to locality and circumstance, of converting barns to museums, an extension of the traditional storage use; to farm shops, an extension of farming activity; to community halls for dancing, sport and meetings; to restaurants; to premises for light industry.

It is put forward in the summary:

> The more a use is able to utilise the whole building as one large space, the less will be the impact on the external appearance of the structural frame – in effect, the architectural and historic integrity of the building. Most public uses display the common advantage of an internal layout centred on one large space. Museum uses are particularly favourable in this respect due to significantly less demand for ancillary accommodation. In addition, it is usually the case that day-lighting is relatively less important to public uses, thus reducing the impact that fenestration can have on external appearance. The major disadvantage is that public uses generate a considerable number of vehicles. . . .

But so, of course, does normal agricultural use. Vehicles of huge size – belonging to the farmer, his contractors, his customers – cause a shuddering disturbance round a farmstead and its outlying buildings; but a sustainable complaint is rarely made by neighbours. The unattractive face of farming has just to be accepted. There remains no doubt for most people that the ideal use for barns is to put them back into the service of farming. Some farmers think so, too, and recent years have seen a growing reluctance to pull barns down. Many, indeed, have made a positive effort to find a better use for them than storing bags of fertilizer (that are anyway waterproof), or rearing a few calves. For business-like storing, the fork-lift truck, which goes easily round obstructions and stacks pallets to a height of 20 feet, has been spoken of as the saviour of barns.

A solution always liable to cause public annoyance is selling for scrap value, or for re-erection complete elsewhere – except in certain circumstances to a museum of old buildings – and proposals for such transactions are not always announced in a local paper as boldly as in 1979 by a farmer of Billingshurst, Sussex, who advertised 'For dismantling and sale, four magnificent barns, all over 400 years old'. None of these barns, of course, had appeared on the Department of the Environment's comparatively short list of barns having 'special architectural or historic interest'.

The listing of any building by one of the Department's inspectors prevents dismantling for any purpose without a public inquiry; the building must continue to exist even if the owner cannot comply with an order to repair, and if it is wilfully damaged or neglected the local authority can compulsorily purchase. In 1981 Braintree District Council

Design for a barn in monastic style, 1830 (Peter Robinson, *Designs for Farm Buildings*)

in Essex acquired in this way a medieval barn at Coggeshall, and a local trust, helped by the Historic Buildings Council, was to replace it at the estimated cost – it includes the buying price – of £250,000. Superficially this barn seems unremarkable with its oak framework, weather-boarding and pegtile roof; the owner had tried hard to get permission to demolish. But it was built in the period of the Crusades and is one of the oldest barns of its kind in Europe.

Listing by no means hinders acceptance of a sensible change of use. In fact a local authority which has enforced the preservation of a barn (so far as this is possible) will be anxious for a function to be found for it. Much depends on the discretion of the officials. One authority at least has refused to sanction a blameless agricultural use, housing heavy machinery, because the elevation would be altered by raising a doorway. The farmer angrily told a meeting of conservationists in 1980 that he had been obliged to build a large new structure to shelter his machines, and had arranged for the inviolate barn to be taken into the guardianship of the Department of the Environment itself on the understanding that they would restore and find a decorous use. Instead, seven years had passed without anything happening and, seeing the barn daily from his bedroom window, the farmer often wished, he said, that he had driven a bulldozer through it.

To be fair to the local authorities, most were readier at the start of the 1980s to permit careful alteration for farming purposes, and to authorize grants to help with the work. A more lenient attitude makes sense in the context of history, for ancient buildings withstood plenty of changes in the past without ceasing to be revered. Consider what happened to farm buildings during the eighteenth century – let alone to hundreds and thousands of houses. The Agricultural Revolution brought some quite new demands for the corn barn, and doorways designed for sheaves delivered by pack-horse were enlarged to let in tall waggons. When this improvement was made to the tithe barn of Buckland Abbey, thereby altering the appearance of a building already venerated, the only complainers were the workmen who strained themselves cutting through the massive stonework.

From Roman times barns have been intended as workplaces as well as for storage, and hundreds of empty ones – alas not yet enough – have found a new purpose in becoming the premises of craftsmen and others making furniture, building boats, fashioning ironwork. Thirty feet of headroom may be a disadvantage, even if craftsmen can appreciate the church-like beauty of the early roof timbering – and so, too, is the darkness: on the credit side, generally water and electricity have already been laid on and the rent is low.

The arrival of such a workshop in a quiet country place stimulates, even though it may be the only hope for the village's continuance, fears of unsightly and noisy expansion – and the recollection that the Morris Cowley Works began in a bicycle shed. Again, the licensing suggestion reported a few pages back seems the answer. Let the local authorities issue annual or bi-annual licences, at least for a preliminary period, instead of being required either to refuse or to grant planning permission. By that means if a business is deemed to have grown too obtrusive for its setting, its tenure of a barn can be terminated – and never mind the agreed terms of compensation.

For everyone interested in extending indefinitely the life of England's old barns there was a hopeful passage in a planning circular of 1980 from the Department of the Environment; it specifically encouraged resort to 'disused agricultural buildings' to ease 'the problems of starting and maintaining small-scale businesses'. Following the near-disastrous fire of 1980 at the Bredon tithe barn in Gloucestershire, it is to be hoped the operatives are careful in handling the coal braziers they light to keep warm.

The amenity societies have been ever busier in recent years all over England, and interestingly their concerns with pleasant scenes have begun to impinge on farmers; but it is difficult to see how it could be otherwise, so active are members in moving about, chatting to strangers and expressing opinions on the look of things.

The conservation movement, in fact, is affecting the very people whose business with the land has been hitherto entirely practical. And as a result farmers in increasing numbers are ready to join non-farmers in considering the visual impact as well as the convenience of farm buildings old and new, and they no longer make it clear that such matters appear to them irrelevant.

Today anyone found repairing and polishing early tractors, getting together a farm museum or patching a sixteenth-century barn is quite likely to be a farmer. Such a man is well aware that his older possessions are worth more, visually and financially, than he had previously thought.

PART TWO

EXAMPLES OF BUILDINGS

Chapter 1

For Livestock

Longhouse, Wales   early eighteenth century

Some of the early buildings for livestock were extended enough to shelter also the farmer and his family. These buildings, now known as longhouses, were still being put up in upland regions in the early eighteenth century; ancient versions have survived in the Lake counties and in the west of England, especially on Dartmoor.

The longhouse drawn has been re-erected at the Welsh Folk Museum, Cardiff. Accommodation for animals was on the left and for human beings and produce on the right. Between the two parts of the building there is a cross-passage, forming a lobby. The first longhouses had no such passage and the farmer went directly from his quarters to those of his animals.

Laithe, North Yorkshire   mid nineteenth century

The buildings of the upland and mainly pastoral zones are more compact than those of mixed farms in the lowlands. The farmer in the hills, whose corn-growing is solely to feed livestock, typically made use of a terrace of chambers known in the north as a laithe.

The laithe drawn has doorways which lead – from left to right – (1) to the byre or cowhouse; (2) to the granary – up the steps; (3) to the carthouse; (4) to the stable; (5) to a small barn. The absence of a fold yard suggests that, as was usual, the cows were always either in the byre or out at pasture.

Laithe house, Vale of York   mid eighteenth century

A laithe house has a farmhouse as well as farm buildings under one roof – the section on the right comprises cowhouses and the dairy. Since there is no direct access to the cattle from the house – access being from the outside, without any cross-passage – this Georgian building of c. 1770 is not technically a longhouse (see previous page).

Stables and barn, Norfolk   late seventeenth, mid eighteenth century

On the left, a stable block with accommodation for carriages. Built in the 1680s, it has the ornamental gable ends which denote Dutch influence. The corn barn built against it on the right is of Georgian date and retains the original ventilation panels of spaced-out bricks. Its end wall out of the drawing has been taken down to allow a combine harvester to be parked inside.

Stables, Kent late seventeenth century

Another brick-built building with pretensions to style – and again a Dutch gable end – where a landowner would keep the horses used by himself and his family. It has one of the fodder lofts which were to be criticized as unhealthy, but this one is placed above a stable so tall that there was enough air for the horses. And the chance of dust falling on them was reduced by there being only one way of reaching the loft, by an outside iron ladder.

74

Farm stable, Kent   mid nineteenth century

Whatever they may be used for today, the old stables for workhorses tend to look more like domestic buildings than any others in a farmstead. They commonly have a central front door and windows of ample size, even the fashionable sash windows. The four-stall stable illustrated has casement windows in cast iron. It is also loft-free.

Horses have long been appreciated as artificial animals which respond to special treatment. J. C. Loudon, writing in the 1830s, at a time when horses were multiplying and when many were ill-treated, informed farmers in both his encyclopedias that there was no animal which delighted more in cleanliness nor more disliked bad smells. Farmers, he said, must be careful to have no hen roost, hog sty or necessary house (outside lavatory) near the stables: the swallowing of feathers by horses had in particular proved injurious. Dogs, fowls and goats should never be permitted to enter their quarters.

Workhorses, he went on, should have ample room.

When it is considered how much the health of almost all quadrupeds depends on their reposing for a portion of every twenty-four hours in a horizontal position, and more especially when we reflect that the horse is particularly liable to have swelled legs and heels, we cannot help being of the opinion that all horses ought to be lodged in separate cells or rooms, with divisions so high as to prevent them from seeing each other.

Farm stable, Lancashire   late nineteenth century

Because of the popularity of riding, England's population of horses is said to be almost as great today as it was at the start of Queen Victoria's reign (when the human population was a third smaller). The number has been added to by a recent re-introduction of horses on a few farms for doing odd jobs.

Although well built, farm stables were less architecturally stylish than stables for riding and carriage horses; the latter indicated status and might resemble a village school or a gymnasium. The stable illustrated has eight stalls, a hayloft and – within the flight of steps leading to this – a kennel for a guard dog.

Most old farm stables date from the middle years of the nineteenth century when the employment of oxen as draught animals was declining; oxen barely needed stabling other than a rough shelter. Contemporary text books, showing a variety of feeding racks and other fittings, stated that stables should be 16 feet wide and allow at least 5 feet between animals. They should be at least 9 feet high for the sake of ventilation and should not have a hay loft over them, because this reduced the flow of air and allowed dust to fall down through cracks in the floorboards.

Horses in low-ceilinged quarters

In practice, farm stables went on being built with an upper floor, usually just above the horses' heads. Lofts were convenient for storing hay, straw and oats near the point of use – and as rough bedrooms for carters. Sometimes a carter would make a private hole in the floor for supplying his particular animal with extra food. 'A handful of oats above the farmer's ration', writes Edith Brill, 'put a gloss on a horse's coat which no amount of grooming could achieve.' Farmers were generally aware of what went on and the practice offered a cast-iron excuse for declining a job to a man whose looks they did not like. A farmer could ask: 'Would you be ready to take a few handfuls of oats from me to keep your horse up to the mark?' 'Yes' was the wrong answer – 'I won't employ a man who would steal from me.' And so was 'No' – 'I won't employ a carter who is not prepared to put his horse first.'

Cowhouse, Kent   late eighteenth century

The cowhouse or byre was for centuries the place where dairy cows were hand milked, loosely tied by the neck, two to a stall. It was the permanent winter quarters, too, for those cows which avoided being slaughtered in the autumn because of lack of food for them. Food troughs were at ground level and hay racks attached to the wall. Water was provided in bowls.

Many existing cowhouses are survivors from the mid nineteenth century. These tend to be better ventilated than their predecessors whose built-in lofts left little headroom and caused the byres to be dark and insanitary.

Cow stall   nineteenth century

The fitting-out of cowhouses varied from farm to farm, but stalls designed for two cows with tethering posts only were usual. Loudon strongly advised partitions between each pair of cows. 'This will in great measure prevent accidents and secure the quiet animals from being injured by the vicious.'

Cattle yard and shelter, Suffolk   mid nineteenth century

Cattle yards with shelters provided the standard accommodation – it was often overcrowded – for the rearing of young stock, especially on mixed farms in East Anglia where there was plenty of straw for the litter. As the animals moved about in the yard, they trod dung into the litter to form manure. However, this byproduct could be spoilt by heavy rain and later in the nineteenth century it became approved practice to cover yards completely the better to conserve the manure.

Linhay, Somerset   mid nineteenth century

Linhay is the West Country word for an open cattle shelter with an equally open upper floor (this being known as a tallet) for storing hay and straw. Such buildings were peculiar to Devon and surrounding counties – and circular pillars, or columns, of rubble stone are typical. They tended to be sited at a distance from the farm where they functioned as isolated manure factories serving the surrounding fields. The linhay shown above is seen to be at present in general agricultural use.

Field barn, Yorkshire   eighteenth century

Small stone buildings designed for animals and fodder strew the uplands of Yorkshire and Derbyshire. In such regions a living is today hard to make by traditional methods and many of the buildings are deserted. But efforts have been made, especially in Derbyshire through the example of the Duchess of Devonshire, to put them at the service of hikers wanting an overnight resting place. The small charge for such use of several empty field barns would make a welcome addition to the income of the farmer, or his wife.

Field barn, Derbyshire early nineteenth century

In the uplands of northern England all barns tend to be plainer structures than the porched threshing barns of the south. The function of the isolated building drawn was to store hay, shelter cattle and to provide a collection point for manure. A typical field barn of the gritstone plateau of Derbyshire, it has a doorway just large enough to permit the quick entry of a hay cart between showers – the small doors lead to cow and calf pens.

Bank barn, Yorkshire   nineteenth century

Bank barns and bank buildings are to be seen in various forms, but in each case the idea was to reduce labour by taking advantage of a slope. Thus there may be a small threshing or hay barn at the upper level into which carts can be wheeled – perhaps up a short ramp – while at the lower level a cowhouse or stable could receive fodder by having it simply dropped through hatches in the floor. The building illustrated has window-like apertures for easy insertion of hay.

Common in the Lake District (and known in Switzerland), the bank barn is a compact example of a farm building designed for more than one purpose. It first appeared in the eighteenth century and was still being put up until 1914 – according to R. W. Brunskill in his book *Vernacular Architecture of the Lake Counties*, 1974.

Smithy, Oxfordshire   mid nineteenth century

Farm horses needed re-shoeing every few months and farmers liked to be within reach of a smithy, or forge. Situated near a crossroads, its forecourt often had a spreading chestnut tree, as in Longfellow's poem, to shade waiting horses and their attendants. Oxen had to be shod, too, though just with two small plates on each foot. An ox could not be taught to lift a foot, so the animal was thrown and roped and two boys sat on its neck while the feet were being tied to a tripod of iron poles. The smithy made a good place for exchanging local news and it drew people who merely wanted to watch. A few of the big estates had their own smithy – equipped with hearth, bellows, anvil, vice and sundry tools – at which a farrier attended on certain days.

Pigsties, Kent   nineteenth century

Pen-and-run pigsties. On sunny days the pigs used to like to sunbathe as well as eat in the run, the walls of which were low enough for passers-by to scratch their backs with sticks. William Marshall advised farmers in the early nineteenth century to provide their pigs with the means to scratch themselves. 'Every sty should have a rubbing post ... the enjoyments of the post are discernible in the animals' looks and in their liveliness and apparent contentment.' Inside the low-roofed pen, suitable for furless animals sensitive to cold, the pigs were comfortable on straw which they normally refrained from fouling.

Sties were new to the eighteenth century. Previously the pig was regarded as an animal of the woodlands where it might forage under the supervision of a village swineherd. It was the growth of butter- and cheese-making which led to pigs being put in houses, to act as profitable consumers of waste dairy products.

Pigsties, Yorkshire   nineteenth century

Pigsties with an upper storey serving as a poultry house, this having its doors on the other side. While the fowls were warmed by the bodies of the pigs below, the pigs were to an extent spared condensation on the ceilings of their quarters by the insulating effect of litter and droppings.

THE URBAN COWHOUSE OF THE
MID NINETEENTH CENTURY

By 1820 London contained about 8000 cows. Urban cowhouses were fronted by a shop selling milk and cream, several of the bigger ones being in the region of Marble Arch. J. C. Loudon, who inspected several urban cowhouses, reported with some distaste on the Metropolitan Dairy in the Edgware Road, counting it as an establishment typical of its kind. The site of this was probably between George Street and Upper Berkeley Street at a point where a London map of 1819 shows Cow Yard. If so, it was obviously still operating in 1857 since a street directory of that date gives against 31 Edgware Road (at the entrance to Cow Yard): Edward Biggs, farmer and cow-keeper and James Hellings, butterman.

In the 1840s J. C. Loudon reported that the Edgware Road cowhouse was intended for 360 cows, most of them in milk but some fattening, and that the space allowed for each cow was about 3 feet 9 inches.

> There is one gutter in the centre and no raised footpath, it being found that the latter is apt to make the cows stumble if turned out on any occasion. It is true these occasions are rare, for the cows are never untied from the day they are put into the milking shed till they are removed to the fattening sheds, or till they are taken out to be sold or to be sent into the country to remain till calving time.

Loudon was displeased by the idea of drinking 'milk chiefly manufactured from grains and distiller's wash, and produced from cows deprived of all exercise in the open air'.

Another documented cowhouse consisted of cellars in Golden Square described thus in 1847:

> forty cows are kept in them, two in each seven feet of space. There is no ventilation save by the unceiled, tiled roof through which the ammoniacal vapours escape . . . there is at one end a large tank for grains, a store place for turnips and another for hay, and between them a receptacle into which the liquid manure drains and the solid is heaped . . . the stench arising is insufferable.

Kentish Town made a more rural source of milk and had plenty of cow-lairs since, with Islington, it was one of the main milk-producing districts for the metropolis; but in the late eighteenth century as more building became necessary, the old names like Church Field and Figs Meade were replaced by Lower Brickfield and Upper Brickfield. Farmers had entered the lucrative business of turning pastures into bricks (Gillian Tindall, *The Fields Beneath*, Granada, 1980).

Chapter 2

For Crops, Processing and Equipment

Tithe barn, Wiltshire   fourteenth century

The huge stone tithe barns, with a formidable timber framework behind the stone, are among the best of the medieval buildings. Most were built on monastic estates and they had to be big to house the church tithes which arrived in the form of actual produce; they also stored the produce of the home farm. Church-like in appearance, monastic tithe barns reflect ecclesiastical wealth and outclass ordinary farm buildings.

Interior   late medieval

Timber-framed, church-like interior of a stone barn in the west of
England. Typically of the west, it has a cruck structure, this type being
known as raised cruck. Note at the end the ventilation opening of
ecclesiastical appearance.

Tithe barn, Worcestershire   thirteenth century

The doorways of medieval tithe barns are less wide than those of later barns because the tithes, the rents in kind and other produce, were less often wheeled in than brought by hand or by horses with panniers. Such barns were magnified versions of ordinary corn barns, having several more bays and at least two threshing floors. Stone flags or smooth timber was the preferred treatment for threshing floors, which were placed between two opposing doors for the sake of the draught. The term tithe barn is sometimes used loosely today, not all of the huge barns having been designed for storage of tithes; at the same time there are moderate sized barns near churches where the parson did store tithes.

Corn barns, Sussex   early eighteenth century

Before railways moved manufactured building materials from one part of the country to another, builders almost invariably took the materials that were to hand. This pair of barns on the Sussex downs is a good example of enduring structures so made. In addition to timber from nearby woods, the components consist of local flint stones from the downs, locally arising sand and lime, and farm-grown straw thatch. Barns where hand-threshing took place are recognizable from the fact that the doors do not reach the ground, the gap of a foot or so being taken up by a plank resting in notches; this was called a spurting board and stopped grain escaping when being flailed and during winnowing when a draught was created to blow away chaff.

Corn barn, Gloucestershire   sixteenth century

A charming example of a Cotswold barn in stone. It has two threshing
floors and two large doors capable of admitting loaded corn waggons
and letting them out through slightly smaller doors the other side.
Porches could be useful for general protection of the interior and also
for the parking of waggons clear of threshing floors. There is a pitching
hole high up on the right; otherwise the only visible openings are
ventilation slits.

Interior   Late mediaeval

Timber-framed interior of a barn in eastern England with aisles and a bricked threshing floor. The construction is post and truss. Note the king posts rising from the tie beams to support the ridge beams at the apex of the roof.

Corn barn, Kent   eighteenth century

By about February each year the typical corn barn would have at one end a stack of unthreshed straw and at the other a stack of empty straw – ready for livestock litter and for thatching. The grain as it accumulated on the threshing floor was taken in sacks to granaries, one of which might be a chamber under the barn roof with a hole placed strategically over an oat roller; seed corn would be carefully segregated. The barn drawn is remarkable for having canopies instead of porches as protection for waggons.

Barn, Yorkshire   early eighteenth century

Some old farm buildings have been so much altered it is hard to classify them, but this one remains a barn, now multipurpose, even though five of the present openings have been carved out of the rubble stone. Originally it had only the round-arched central doorway: unlike the other openings, this has been fashioned with neatly executed voussoirs and quoins. Although not very wide, the entrance was enough to admit a pony with panniers. Barns were widely adapted to house cattle in the late nineteenth century, when most farmers found it no longer paying to grow corn as a cash crop, and let their fields turn from brown to green.

Double corn barn, Cambridgeshire   late eighteenth century

A traditional large barn which was one of the last of its type to be built. Barns were to become smaller – according, of course, to acreage. Apart from the fact that the corn sheaves were increasingly being dried in the stack yard, instead of in the barn, it was apparent that mechanical threshing was going to reduce the storage space required.

However, the introduction of the powered threshing machine was slow – and at least a small threshing floor was retained in case it broke down – and as late as the 1830s J. C. Loudon was offering such advice to flailers as that they 'should wear thin-soled shoes to avoid bruising the grains'.

The flail was a leather-jointed stick, the part for beating the sheaves being half the length of the other. Two men flailed together, striking in turn at a heap of about a dozen sheaves. The straw was raked off when the loose corn below was about a foot high. In the absence of winnowing machines, one way of separating the chaff was to open the doors and throw the corn up and down in the breeze. A few farmers continued hand flailing until the Second World War and Marie Hartley found a small-time Yorkshire farmer doing so, as a matter of course, in 1967. He appears photographed in her book, with Joan Ingilby, *Life in the Moorlands of North-East Yorkshire*, 1972.

Corn barn, Suffolk   eighteenth century

A thatched barn of brick which has suffered from the lateral thrust of grain and other produce piled up inside: the end wall has recently been stabilized with steel tie rods and wooden buttresses. Before the introduction of Portland cement the bricks in a brick wall were bedded rather than stuck together by the lime mortar between them. In domestic buildings, where there was no comparable outward pressure, gravity, or weight, was enough to hold such walls upright.

Even the elaborate brick barns erected by Thomas Coke at Holkham had to be carefully loaded to avoid bursting. Even so cracks are to be seen. When loose grain is to be stored today in an old brick barn, internal containing walls, or huge metal container-linings may be constructed.

Barn, Humberside   eighteenth century

A small northern barn – note the slits for ventilating stored corn sheaves – which has been adapted to house livestock and given an upper floor for fodder. The shed built on to the left has been variously used – recently as a root store and an implement shelter.

Wheelhouse, Northumberland   *early nineteenth century*

Andrew Meikles's invention of the threshing machine in 1784 necessitated a new kind of farm building for sheltering the horse or horses which provided the power. Wheelhouses – also called engine sheds and gin sheds – were ideally airy places. In them horses trod a circular path, turning round a bar which operated by means of an overhead crown wheel and pinion the driving shaft of the threshing machine, which was situated on the other side of a wall, in the barn.

These harmless-looking buildings, round, square or several sided, represented for many in the nineteenth century a disturbing advance in the mechanization of farm work which was taking away winter-time work. In southern parts of England especially, the construction of a wheelhouse against a barn alerted discontented farm workers to the presence of a smashable threshing machine. Many were destroyed. But after about 1850 the farmer who had bought a threshing machine could avoid drawing attention to it by hiring a portable horse engine: this had a drive shaft which lay flat on the ground, and had to be stepped over by the horse as it went round. These were known as sweep engines, and a few were still in service on the 1930s.

Wheelhouse, Northumberland   mid nineteenth century

Northumberland is the great county for wheelhouses. It contained about 500 in 1870 and only a little less than half that number remain today – mostly as general-purpose sheds. Few traces of the machinery they housed still exist outside museums, but the hole in the barn wall which the drive shaft went through is always to be seen.

The threshing machine, when it ceased to cause violent feelings, so speeded the release of corn that a big stack could be dealt with in a day, and it reduced by about 15 per cent the corn generally lost during hand threshing – roughly the amount used annually as seed. But the hand threshers lost even more in bad seasons when the grain was hard to loosen from the ear. 'Before the invention of the threshing machine,' wrote Sir John Sinclair in *The Code of Agriculture*, 1831, 'the large corn farmer . . . had trouble, vexation and loss from careless and wicked servants.' However, threshing machines had to be fed thinly with the corn sheaves: otherwise sudden jerks and strains injured the horses and caused breakdowns.

Wheelhouse and (on left) Dutch barn, Northumberland
mid nineteenth century

A good horse exerted a pull of about 170 lb on his chain and normally at least two horses were yoked in the wheelhouse – as many as six are known to have been used. Irregularities in the power they provided were largely removed after 1830 by a new way of yoking invented by a Scottish blacksmith. The effect of this was that if one horse relaxed the other immediately pressed the collar to his shoulders.

Wheelhouse, Yorkshire   early nineteenth century

Some farmers regarded the wheelhouse as a place for breaking in a young horse; when put to work with experienced animals the young horse would be led by a halter and have a rope round his belly to obviate lying down. Sometimes new horses grew dizzy and had to be rested, but although the work was monotonous and set up a loud rattling noise, horses grew to so like the team work that often, when released from the plough, they would make straight for the wheelhouse.

Wheelhouse for oxen   early nineteenth century

This is part of the model farmstead in Sussex shown on page 139 and depicts a wheelhouse formerly operated by oxen. The houses in which oxen were simply sheltered had a door wider than that of stables to accommodate the horns.

Barn with steam engine, Yorkshire   mid nineteenth century

The new and hefty power of steam began to replace animal power for threshing about 1840. Fixed steam engines called for a tall chimney to produce a good draught for the fire to carry away smoke. J. C. Loudon was worried that brick chimney shafts would disfigure the countryside.

> We would strongly recommend some attention to elegance of form in these very conspicuous parts of a modern farmery. The public has surely the right to expect that they should be built in what is considered good taste, no less than spires of churches.

Barn with water wheel, Denbighshire   early nineteenth century

Water power for driving the threshing machine cannot be said to have succeeded the horse engine because it was always known to be the superior method where a suitable supply of water existed, or could be brought without excessive labour. The wheel illustrated is of the undershot variety and impelled by the passage of water at the bottom.

'By means of water,' wrote Robert Brown in 1811, in his *Treatise on Rural Affairs*, 'the business of threshing is executed speedily, completely and economically.' J. C. Loudon in the 1830s described with approval a machine that could be driven either by water or by four horses.

> Advantage may be taken of water when it is abundant, while in dry seasons the horses can be applied. . . . By the simple operation of varying the positions of the pinions on the shaft, threshing may be carried on without interruption either with the water or the horses separately; or a small quantity of water may be applied to assist the horses at any time, when a sufficient supply of water cannot be obtained to impel the machine alone.

Granary, Wiltshire   early seventeenth century

Since the late seventeenth century specially built granaries held those parts of the farmer's crop which were to be preserved as food for his family and for his animals, and also as seed for the following year's crops: the space was divided into large wooden bins. Granaries as grain-storage places additional to the barn became common in the eighteenth century and many sat on mushroom shaped stones (staddles) to discourage entry by rats and mice. However, some farmers long maintained the old practice of storing grain upstairs in the farmhouse.

The granary drawn is built over a general store in a building supported by raised timber crucks – the stone is infilling. Unsophisticated cruck construction had been a West Country tradition since the Middle Ages. Granaries well away from damp ground and vermin were always preferred. The floor had its planks fitting as tightly as possible, the walls and ceiling were generally whitewashed and the windows had louvred strips of board for ventilation. In the floor there might be a trap door, supplied with a windlass, for the easy service of processing machinery below.

Granary, Worcestershire   late eighteenth century

A granary of box-frame construction resting on brick columns to form beneath it a cart shelter, a common arrangement. The small arched openings in the flight of steps lead to kennels for guard dogs. Grain was a farm produce to be defended against pilferers of all sorts and access for mice-eating owls was encouraged. Some of the early monastic granaries incorporated a cell in which a monk-on-duty spent the night.

Taking grain up to the granary was one of the heaviest farm jobs. Relays of men toiled up the steps with each a two-hundredweight sack on his back. The trips were not complete on reaching the granary, for the men had then to walk up a plank laid against the growing pile before tipping out their loads.

Dutch barns, Yorkshire   nineteenth century

Skeleton buildings of timber for storing hay or straw. Examples still exist in the Vale of York and are impressive against a skyline, but repeated losses of the clay tiles to the wind have hastened demolition. They are farm-made versions of the more familiar Dutch barn (see page 102) which has metal or concrete supports and a rounded corrugated iron roof.

Open shelters for hay were copied from the Netherlands in the sixteenth century; the original version had a roof that moved up and down on poles to accommodate more or less hay, but the mechanism often went wrong. As the value of hay and straw rose in the 1860s farmers in wet districts increasingly acquired Dutch barns as an alternative to building and thatching stacks. The *Journal of the Royal Agricultural Society* was strongly recommending them in the 1880s and Stephens's *Book of the Farm*, 1889 edition, reported that iron versions were plentiful. Even at that time it was possible to buy them prefabricated.

Waggon shed, Kent   early nineteenth century

Waggon sheds had no doors. They were designed merely to protect carts and other valuable farm implements from the worst of the weather; wood-jointed implements were in special need of some protection from sun and rain. The simplest buildings on a farmstead, they were generally faced away from the farmstead, or stood separate from the other buildings near the farm gate for ease of access. When so placed, cattle were not likely to get in and do damage.

The example drawn here was originally a very simple structure. The sections on either side of the entrance are later additions, the roofs being carried down to shelter them in a manner typical of Kent. These extensions were used for many years for the accommodation of pigs.

Oasthouse, Kent   c. 1820

Hop flowers were being dried in the sixteenth century for the flavouring and clearing of beer, and generally they were dried in the sun or slowly on the floors of any convenient shed. The purpose-built oasthouses which are so familiar today in the south-east corner of England date from the last years of the eighteenth century. As well as drying the hops and storing them, the oasthouse made a social centre, until the 1950s, for the parties of pickers who arrived in September.

Oasthouses, known in Worcestershire, abound in Kent because Kent was the county to which Dutch emigrants first introduced hops as a cash crop. The tower of an oasthouse, the kiln, was at first square but became round from about 1810, this shape being supposed to give a better circulation of heat. From the late nineteenth century it was square again to fit in with an improved method of moving hops in and out of the drying area next door.

Double oasthouse, Kent   early nineteenth century

In its day the direct-heating oasthouse was the most scientific of all farm buildings – a better way of drying any crop with artificial heat was not developed until the 1930s. The kiln had a central fireplace at ground level. Half way up the kiln there was a slatted floor on which the hop flowers were strewn to a depth of about 9 inches. As outside air was drawn in through holes at the base of the kiln, the hot air of the fire rose, taking with it by-products of combustion, these inevitably tainting the hops to some extent even though they rested on a hair blanket. The cowl at the top helped to sustain a strong draught. To produce as little smoke as possible the oasthouse foreman arranged for the coke or coal fire to be burning red before the hops were spread out. Charcoal made the ideal fuel.

Only a few oasts were built to dry by means of indirect heating. These had an enclosed grate, the heat from which was released by means of a flue twisting below the drying floor. Although hops so dried ('Pure Air Dried') fetched a slightly higher price, the extra cost of construction was greater and the drying time longer. The inventor of the indirect method is said to have been John Read, a Sussex gardener with experience of heating greenhouses with smoke flues.

Oasthouse   late nineteenth century

After being dried over the fire the hops were moved into the upper floor of the adjacent barn-like structure and pushed into long sacks known as pockets. From there the men despatched them, following a cooling period, through a trap door to the ground floor for storage until used.

Early in the twentieth century power-driven fans – puller and pusher – were introduced, and as soon as engineers discovered how to regulate the draught, cowls were no longer needed. Thus it came about that from the 1930s hops have been dried by oil-fired burners in sheds as plain as those in which natural drying took place in the seventeenth century. A few farmers continued to use the traditional oasts, but no one still built them. Many oasthouses have been converted for dwellings.

Corn bins, Suffolk   mid twentieth century

As corn came to be no longer dried by sun and wind, so cornstacks were rarely seen by about 1960, and drying installations had to be brought into service to cope with the sudden mass of corn produced by the combine harvester. Some have been set up in barns.

The metal, top-loaded corn bins shown here between Victorian buildings dry their contents by air blown through under pressure. This system may be contrasted with the storing of undried grain in airtight silos, the formation of carbon dioxide killing unwelcome germs. Grain so treated is unsuitable, though, for flour or seed, and must be fed only to livestock.

THE ROOT HOUSE OF THE
MID NINETEENTH CENTURY

The root harvest for the winter feeding of cattle, an eighteenth-century introduction, was often clamped – that is, stored in big heaps protected by earthing over – but a section of a building was also used where convenient, for such things as turnips, potatoes and mangel-wurzels.

The root house, said Loudon,

> should always join the cattle sheds and communicate with them by an inner door that opens into the feeder's walk by the heads of the cattle. The entrance ought to be so large as to admit a loaded cart. . . . The master should be careful that the yard man keeps such places perfectly clean and sweet in order that the roots need contact no bad smell, as cattle are in many cases extremely nice in their feeding and, when once disgusted with any sort of food, seldom take to it again in a proper manner.

In the 1930s roots were still commonly being harvested in the age-old way, by hand labour. Adrian Bell writing of his farming experiences in *The Cherry Tree* called it 'a scrabbling, humble, earthen affair with none of the poise and joviality of pitching the corn'.

Chapter 3

For Auxiliary Purposes

Covered well, Surrey   early nineteenth century

From the earliest times farms have had to be sited where there was water, and even today farmers do not always care to rely entirely on piped supplies. For a supply of clean water wells were dug; and the sort of windlass shown here, with wheels and pinions, eased the job of lifting the water by bucket.

For the necessary work there were travelling well-diggers. A usual method on their part, according to Loudon in his *Encyclopaedia of Agriculture*, was to lay a ring of flat boards on the intended site and build on them a circular brick wall about 6 feet high. Once the mortar had set, a man got inside and by careful digging away at the earth allowed the wall to sink. By stages more brickwork could be added to the wall and it became a well-lining. The other way of doing the job, building up from the bottom could have been by comparison hard and hazardous work.

It might be necessary to go down 250 feet for a reliable source of clean water, but where all that was needed was a well slowly filled by surface seams, a depth of 20 feet was often enough. Once over 30 feet, hand-pump pressure would not operate to raise water.

Loudon recorded an accident in digging a well at a point 30 feet from the Thames in Chelsea. The digger was some 200 feet down, preparing his way past the side of the tool. He scarcely had time to withdraw the borer, pick up his other tools and be drawn up to the top. The water soon rose 200 feet.

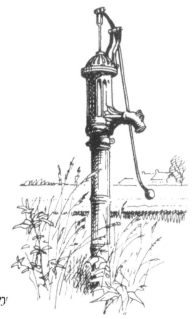

Common pump   late nineteenth century

If you are overheated and need some cold water, to come upon a pump like this can be a delight. In the nineteenth century many villages relied on the local brook as the source of water for all purposes, but sooner or later farmers would tap it for their animal-watering ponds and a muddy trickle became an annoyance to the local people. This happened at the Cambridgeshire village of Foxton and there was much rejoicing when a benefactor had bores sunk and pumps installed at every farmhouse, thus ensuring a supply of pure water (Roland Parker, *The Common Stream*, 1975).

Cast iron pumps are still often seen at farmsteads, operating by means of suction and a leather washer. There is not always a well underneath because where water exists in a particular stratum – provided it is within 30 feet of the surface – it can be drawn up readily by a hand pump. It is only necessary to let a pipe down to the requisite depth.

In *Cottage, Farm and Villa Architecture*, J. C. Loudon shows an early nineteenth-century pump similar to the one drawn and he writes: 'As fixtures belonging to the farmery . . . we include a pump. The most suitable kind for farmeries is that of cast iron which, according to the bore, may be had at various prices from £2 upwards, the total price depending on the length of tube required to reach the bottom.' Pumps long continued important. So late as 1930, only a third of England's farms had access to a piped water supply.

Donkey wheel, Kent   seventeenth century

The donkey wheel as a means of lifting water met a special need common to the chalk hills of south-east England. In this region rainfall is rapidly absorbed and soon sinks. Before the days of a mains water supply, wells of up to 300 feet in depth had to be sunk by communities and farms on the higher hills in order to reach the water level. The common pump was useless where the water was over 30 feet deep, and getting buckets up and down such wells by hand was a laborious and lengthy job which wooden treadmills powered by animals could accomplish with ease.

The wheel drawn is at Eggarton in Kent – and so well balanced that even today it revolves at a touch. It raises water from a well 100 feet deep; the water is delivered into a stone tank and from there it used to be distributed to a farmyard by gravity. As with all such wheels, a little care is needed in operation: a man who trod this wheel after dining with the proprietor found himself upside down.

Treadwheels operated by human beings or animals were common in

Roman times and still being constructed in England in the late nine-teenth century – so writes Hugo Brunner, to whom I am grateful for permission to draw on an article of his in *Country Life*, 28 December, 1972. The use of donkey wheels for drawing water was first recorded in 1587, he says; and they must have become widespread, since more than 50 examples are recorded, mostly in the Chilterns and the North and South Downs but also as far afield as Devon and Yorkshire. According to a survey by Mr Brunner, twenty-seven still existed in 1972, and at Carisbrooke Castle there was still a treadwheel being worked by donkeys. However, in 1980 Mr Brunner told me that another donkey wheel had been discovered, bringing the number of survivors to twenty-eight.

These surviving wheels vary in size from 10 to 19 feet in diameter, according to the kind of animal that was to drive them. The donkey was the commonest, but horses, retriever dogs and men were used. Children enjoyed doing it. Richard D'Acres in *The Art of Water-Drawing*, 1650 (quoted by Mr Brunner) refers to great hollow wheels in which men tread 'but which are worked more efficiently by cattle and brute beasts'. Donkey wheels were mostly erected in purpose-built well houses among farm buildings.

House for a donkey wheel, Kent   seventeenth century

The bucket would be at the end of a rope leading directly from the wheel's axle, and Mr Brunner quotes Thomas Baskerville writing in 1681 about the wheel at Ashridge Park in Hertfordshire: As soon as the bucket came above the collar of the well a man emptied it into a leaden cistern and at that moment 'the horse turns itself in the wheel without bidding or forcing and travels the other way to draw up the next bucket, and so this water after it has served all the offices of the house runs into the pond.' A refinement elsewhere were two iron hooks attached to the cistern which caught the buckets and automatically tipped them over.

Brakes were generally needed to prevent the bucket from returning rapidly to the bottom of the well. A variety were designed for this purpose, some applied to the axle, some across the outside of the treads and others, in the form of metal straps, to part of the circumference of the wheel. The basic design of the wheel is much like that of water wheels, though generally the construction is lighter, and the disposition of the spokes has of course to allow for the donkey to enter the wheel.

The same principle of the treadwheel used as a crane to lift weights has been applied, writes Mr Brunner, to other purposes, especially for building. Several of England's great churches have a treadwheel above the crossing. In 1963 the treadwheel at Canterbury Cathedral was used to lift a new electric organ into position, while the one at Beverley Minster raises and lowers building materials.

Hydraulic pumping station   c. 1900

A water-driven, water-pumping station operated by a 10-foot iron wheel which drove a three-cylinder pump. Built over a small river, its purpose was not to lift water from a depth below ground but to convey it from a shallow, stream-fed well to a reservoir half a mile away and 120 feet higher up. The reservoir water gravitated to two farms and a village.

This water wheel is of the undershot type, worked by water shooting along the floor of the channel in which the wheel must revolve. The overshot kind, turned by a weight of water falling from above, is more powerful. However, undershot wheels have the advantage of needing no mill pool to provide a head of water: they do need a weir and flood gates to control the flow, for if the level of water is allowed to reach axle height, the wheel just stops going round.

Wind-operated pump for water, Oxfordshire   early 20th century

A fully metal structure with a small set of sails which, on being swiftly turned by the wind, activated a pump for water, although the water ran to waste until the sails were securely braked. The corner of an ancient stone barn on the left is a most pleasing building whose large square threshing machine was still inside in 1981.

Ash-house, Devon   eighteenth century

In parts of the West Country wood ash was thought of highly as a fertilizer and round stone ash-houses with corbelled roofs (to reduce risk of fire) were once common in Devon and Cornwall. Some farmers were able to acquire wood ash from cottagers in return for helping them cart home from a common their winter supply of firewood. The fertilizing properties of the ash might be improved by mixing it with farmyard dung. Kay Coutin has noted in *Devon's Traditional Buildings*, 1978, that a hen roost was sometimes put up in an ash-house for the benefit of the droppings. As well as being spread on the land, ash was useful as a cleansing agent in laundry work.

Lime kiln, Devon   early nineteenth century

A lime kiln which has been given a Gothic look with castellations round the top and pointed arches for its openings; within these are situated the fire holes of the actual kiln. The method for producing calcined lime – which is spread on sour land – was to tip in at the top alternate loads of lime rock and coal. In due course the end product could be raked out of the holes at the bottom. Wherever possible advantage was taken of a hill site to provide a ramp for wheeling up the materials for loading.

Because of the great heat created during burning, it was usual to bury kiln chambers inside a massive box of stone or brick: this was, though, rarely so architectural in appearance as the one illustrated. Remains of lime kilns are to be seen in the limestone areas of the Lake District and in south Devon. A farm textbook, *The Farm*, of 1847 informed young bailiffs that knowing how to construct lime kilns 'on true principles' was properly in their province.

Bee-house, Yorkshire early nineteenth century

The object of the so-called bee-house (it was included in J. C. Loudon's list of farm buildings) was protection against bad weather and theft. In the days before heavy wooden hives, introduced in the 1880s, bees were kept in straw skeps: and these were easily damaged by rain and, being light, were liable to be carried off by thieves. A bee-house normally amounted to no more than a series of recesses in a sunny wall – which might be the wall of the building. 'In front', wrote Loudon, 'there may be either a grated iron door or several horizontal iron bars to lock, so as to permit the free ingress and egress of the bees and yet prevent any person taking them out.' The bee-house illustrated dates from 1832 and is unusually elaborate and attractive. A photograph of it appears in the book by Marie Hartley and Joan Ingilby, *Life in the Moorlands of North-East Yorkshire.*

Dovecote, Somerset   eleventh century

A dovecote of the type believed to have been introduced by the Normans. According to A. O. Cooke in his *A Book of Dovecotes*, 1920, the type became universal, 'a circular and very massive building having walls three feet or more in thickness and a low-domed, vaulted roof'. The latter was at first open in the centre providing a round hole to admit light and air as well as pigeons. Although dovecotes were decorative buildings only found on the estates of the privileged, they served a serious agricultural purpose in providing quantities of food in the winter when fresh meat was scarce. The cooks of a medieval Lord Berkeley handled 2,151 pigeons a year, it is stated by W. H. R. Curtler in his *Short History of English Agriculture*, 1909.

Interior of a dovecote

The walls were lined with hundreds of nesting boxes, a revolving ladder being built in for taking the young birds and for cleaning out. Despite the depredations to corn crops and to thatched roofs over a wide area, some people were still rearing pigeons as a farm crop in the nineteenth century. Eliza Acton wrote in *Modern Cookery*, 1845:

'If extremely young, the birds will be ready in twelve hours for the spit . . . roast them at a brisk fire, keeping them well and constantly basted with butter. Serve with brown gravy and a tureen of parsley and butter.' She also recommended the cook sometimes to 'dish them on young watercress'.

Dovecote, Worcestershire   seventeenth century

A dovecote with 700 nesting boxes; it originally had a four-gabled roof, the present roof being a Georgian alteration. At the end of the seventeenth century it was estimated that England contained about 26,000 dovecotes and that the pigeons ate six million quarters of grain annually. Amid much annoyance, farmers employed boys to drive pigeons from their fields. Under an Act of George III's time, tenant farmers were forbidden to erect dovecotes without a licence from the lord of the manor.

The dovecote illustrated above may be seen at the Avoncroft Museum.

Dovecote in barn, Gloucestershire   seventeenth century

The gable end of a barn full of corn hardly seems a good place to house hundreds of grain-eating pigeons. But the dovecote shown here is of course self-contained and, further, a farmyard where the poultry fore-gathered made a suitable pecking ground for pigeons, too.

Dovecote, Kent   early eighteenth century

A sturdy brick dovecote built in 1703. Set on a slope, it forms a bank
building in that the door to the interior of the pigeons' quarters, where
nesting boxes line the walls, is entered at the other side almost at ground
level. In the lower storey there is, unusually, accommodation for pigs.
The ceiling of the piggery probably gained more in insulation from straw
and droppings on the floor above than the dovecote gained in warmth
from the pigs below.

Chapter 4

Farmsteads

Farmstead, Nottinghamshire   early nineteenth century

With the Enclosure Movement there came the need for new farmsteads away from the villages, and by the 1760s Georgian architects had devised for landowners a neat layout of joined-together farm buildings for mixed farms. Given the reliance of those times on hand labour, the standard Georgian farmstead was both convenient and pleasingly regular in appearance. It was copied, with modifications, for at least a century.

According to the stock pattern, all the buildings were fitted together to make ranges which surround three sides of a square forming a farmyard where the cattle could exercise themselves, and where manure could be allowed to accumulate. The tallest building, the barn, was invariably in the north range to give shelter to the south-facing yard; the two wings leading from the north range contained a collection of animal buildings. In a sense, the farming process began in the stack yard on the far side of the barn. Into this came corn sheaves and out of the adjacent barn came grain to make bread with and straw to serve the animals. Out of the animal houses came straw turned into manure to help grow more crops. The farmhouse was set slightly apart to the south. Even today, the Georgian farmstead plan dominates most farms: a few are barely altered despite the lack of the many hands formerly available.

Farmstead, Gloucestershire seventeenth century

On the left, a barn of traditional Cotswold type which has been usefully extended on either side of the porch. The building to its right, built up against the gable end, is the granary. Beneath this is the wagon shelter, the great stone pillars of which are a familiar feature of such buildings in the west of England. The posture of the two men, who appear to be waiting for something to happen, is a reminder of the fact that in former times the work of the day would not start until the farmer or his bailiff had unlocked the various doors of the farmstead.

Farmstead, Kent   seventeenth century

A yard bounded on two sides by a double threshing barn indicates a large acreage under wheat. However, new ways of managing a farm have often caused a change of use for barns and as far back as the eighteenth century farmers were converting, or part-converting, corn barns for the raising of calves and for housing cattle in winter. A source of spring water often determined the site of a farmstead. But a spring-fed pond in a yard to be used by cattle, as above, could easily become a liability from fouling with manure – often urine would get diverted accidentally and drain straight into it.

Farmstead, Gloucestershire eighteenth century

A farmstead of Cotswold limestone whose parts – barn, granary, cowhouse, stable and carthouse – have accumulated over generations, though with a result that is not in this case without order and local convenience. Because of the use of traditional materials and designs, the individual buildings are impossible to date. A prime function of any farmyard was to be a repository for manure, two heaps of which may be noted above.

Farmstead, Yorkshire   eighteenth century

A group of farm buildings with yard which accommodate, from left to
right, pigs and poultry (the entrance to the poultry house is up some
steps on the other side) and then either horses or cattle. What appear to
be windows high up on the wall of the stable block (it has shown a
tendency to bulge) are pitching holes for delivering fodder. The
chimney on the far right, by the Dutch barn, was probably to do with
boiling up raw scraps for the pigs and hens.

Farmyard, West Sussex   eighteenth century

A common juxtaposition of buildings round a mixed farmyard – here stone and brick with a plain-tiled roof. On the left is the stable, now a cowhouse, with skylit loft above in which many a labourer will have spent the night. This is approached by a flight of stone steps which lead also, by means of the common door, to the granary on the right. Up these steps men used to carry 2-hundred-weight sacks of grain to tip and pile on the granary floor. At right angles to this range is an open cattle shelter into which young stock might walk in and out at will.

Farmstead, Sussex   early nineteenth century

A model farmstead with the yard bounded on three sides by uninter-rupted building. The prominent and unusual barn dominates the north range, the other two ranges, which form a square, comprising small houses for livestock and storage. Built in 1810, this farmstead was still in operation for mixed farming in 1980, the only marked change being a partially covered yard for the protection from rain of manure, animals and vehicles.

The barn marks an early nineteenth-century break with the tradition-al barn with its huge doors for loaded waggons. Corn at this farm was stored in the sheaf under thatch in a stack yard behind, and the purpose of the barn was mechanized threshing on the ground floor; the threshing machine was formerly operated by a wheel turned by oxen – the wheelhouse is just to the right of the barn – and the storage of grain loose on the upper floor. This is reached not by being carried but by being blown in through a tube.

The signs of Regency taste – the low-pitched roofs with jutting out eaves, round arches surrounding recessed brickwork, rudimentary pilasters – are accompanied by Regency economies over building materials. The brick walls are much thinner than they look and not bonded from front to back, so that on the inside cheap bricks are seen, now the plaster has fallen away, to be rough bricks thrown into place. As a result the building has had to be held together with steel rods (note the S pieces) to contain the effects of loose grain thrusting sideways.

Farmstead, Lancashire   nineteenth century

A small farmstead in local stone and brick which is typical of the upland areas where pastoral farms predominate and produce milk for the great industrial conurbations. They are thus unlike corn or mixed farms and have few buildings.

The rear of the farmhouse is seen. If it has not exactly turned its back on the farmstead, as usually happened, it has front windows on the other side which enjoy an uninterrupted view of grassland. The demand for liquid milk from the sprawling towns became so great in the late nineteenth century that dairy farmers on the hills survived the great depression where many other farmers did not.

Farmstead, Suffolk   nineteenth century

Another group which has grown up haphazardly according to changing needs – a typical East Anglian farmstead for a small farm. The farmer remarked that it was all redundant really, but despite the presence of modern buildings elsewhere on the farm, all these old ones were in agricultural use in 1980, the barn housing large vehicles and other machinery and the cartshed containing a variety of implements.

Multi-purpose building   late twentieth century

The old way of concentrating several kinds of animal under one roof, together with products of the field, re-emerges with today's umbrella building of steel, concrete and asbestos sheets. Such buildings are so designed that partitions are easily put up, and easily removed, to accommodate farming needs as they arise. Provision for the farmhouse itself is excluded. The buildings are in fact fully covered farmyards which may be cleared of debris by mechanical means. The example drawn represents a type supplied by the firm of Atcost.

Glossary

Anaerobic storage   confining in the absence of free oxygen to cause
  biochemical change
Aisle   outshut without a partition
Bay   division of a building between upright structural members, traditionally
  wide enough for two oxen
Chaff   husks of corn as threshed or winnowed, cut hay or straw
Churn   large metal milk can
Cob   mixture of earth, chalk, straw and water laid on with fork to make walls
Column   large round body used as decorative support for roof
Combine harvester   self-propelled machine which cuts and reaps corn in one
  mobile act
Corbel   projection from the face of a wall supporting a weight
Cowcake   feed for animals consisting of compressed oils and
  vegetable matter
Cowl   cover for oast tower which moves with the wind to draw up smoke
Cross-passage   in longhouses a passage from front to back dividing animals'
  quarters from those of human beings
Cruck   timber frame using pair of curved timbers rising from ground level
Drill   ridge with seed or growing plants in it
Dry stone wall   wall of stones without benefit of mortar
Ferme ornés   parkland with ornamental buildings
Fodder   food supplied to animals
Fold yard   open yard in which animals are free to move about and
  produce manure
Gable end   vertical wall at end of a pitched roof – Dutch gable has
  curved outline
Kiln   large oven for drying, baking, calcining
King post   perpendicular beam in frame of a roof
Loose housing   keeping cattle untied and free in large cattle shed
Louvre   slatted unglazed window for ventilation

Outshut   projection of a building under same roof
Pantile   tile made in S form
Pillar   support for a building in the form of any kind of post
Pitching hole   opening for flinging out hay, straw, corn, etc.
Post and truss   box frame in which roof trusses rest on a structure of upright
    posts and horizontal beams
Prefabricate   make in standardized parts beforehand
Queen post   one of two upright posts resting on tie beam and
    supporting rafters
Rendering   plastering of outside walls
Rick   stack or heap usually of hay or straw
Silo   airtight chamber for storing grain, etc.
Spinney   small clump of trees
Spruce   type of fir tree
Stack yard   yard for stacks or ricks
Stretcher   brick placed with its length parallel to line of wall
Studs   upright timbers used in timber-framed buildings
Tie rod   rod serving as tie between two walls
Voussoir   one of wedge-like stones that form an arch
Wattle and daub   wall of thin laths or wattles interwoven and plastered over
Weather-boarding   overlapping horizontal boards on outside of a building
Whey   the watery part of milk separated from the curd
Whin   gorse or furze
Winnowing   separating the chaff by wind, as from a fan

Bibliography

Addy, S. O., *Evolution of the English House*, 1933.
Agriculture, Board of, *General View of Agriculture 1793–1815*.
Anon., *The Farm*, Knight's Industrial Library, 1847.
Armstrong, J. *Traditional Buildings accessible to the Public*, Longman, 1967.
Astor, Viscount, *British Agriculture*, Penguin, 1939.
Barley, M. *The English Farmhouse and Cottage*, Routledge & Kegan Paul, 1961.
Bell, A., *The Cherry Tree*, Bodley Head, 1932.
Birch, J. *Stables*, 1892.
Blair, P., *Anglo-Saxon England*, Cambridge University Press, 1956.
Bourne, G. *A Farmer's Life*, Cape, 1927.
Brill, E., *Life and Traditions in the Cotswolds*, Dent, 1973.
Brown, R., *Treatise on Rural Affairs*, 1811.
Brunskill, R., *The Illustrated Handbook of Vernacular Architecture*, Faber, 1971.
Brunskill, R., *Vernacular Architecture of the Lake Counties*, Faber, 1974.
Burnard, R., *Dartmoor Pictorial Records*, 1893.
Caird, Sir J., *English Agriculture in 1850–1*.
Clifton-Taylor, A., *The Pattern of English Building*, Faber, 1972.
Cobbett, W., *Rural Rides*, 1830.
Cooke, A., *A Book of Dovecotes*, 1920.
Coutin, K., Farm Buildings Section of *Devon's Traditional Buildings*,
    Devon County Council, 1978.
Curtler, W., *A Short History of English Agriculture*,
    Oxford University Press, 1909.
Darley, G., *The National Trust Book of the Farm*, Weidenfeld & Nicolson, 1981.
Defoe, D., *A Tour Thro' the Whole Island of Great Britain*, 1727.
Denton, J., *The Farm Homesteads of England*, 1863.
Eden, F., *The State of the Poor*, 1797.
Enock, A., *This Milk Business*, Lewis, 1943.
Ernle, R., *English Farming Past and Present*, Longman, 1912.
Essex County Council, *Historic Barns: a planning appraisal*, 1979.
Ewart, J., *Treatise on the Arrangement of Agricultural Buildings*, 1851.

Ewart Evans, J., *Ask the Fellow who cut the Hay*, Faber, 1956.
Fitzherbert, A., *Boke of Husbondrye*, 1523.
Fussell, G., *Old English Farming Books 1523–1730*, Crosby Lockwood, 1947.
Fussell, G., *More Old English Farming Books 1731–1793*, Crosby Lockwood, 1948.
Garratt, G., *Hundred Acre Farm*, Longmans, 1928.
Gunn, E., *Farm Buildings*, H. C. Long, 1935.
Haggard, H. Rider, *Rural England*, 1898.
Hammond, J. and B., *The Village Labourer*, Longman, 1911.
Harrison, W., Contribution to *Holinshed's Chronicle*, 1577.
Hartley, M. and Ingilby, J., *Life in the Moorlands of North-East Yorkshire*, Dent, 1972.
Harris, R., *Discovering Timber-framed Buildings*, Shire, 1978.
Harvey, N., *A History of Farm Buildings in England and Wales*, David & Charles, 1970.
Harvey, N., *Old Farm Buildings*, Shire, 1975.
Harvey, N., *Farms and Farming*, Shire, 1977.
Harvey, N., *The Industrial Archeology of Farming in England and Wales*, Batsford, 1980.
Henderson, G., *The Farming Ladder*, 1964.
Hewett, C. A., *Historic Barns*, 1979.
Hill, B. and Kempson, R., *Farm Buildings Capital in England and Wales*, Wye College, 1977.
Huggett, F., *A Short History of Farming*, Macmillan, 1970.
Hussey, C., *The Picturesque*, Putnam, 1927.
Jefferies, R., *Hodge and His Masters*, 1880.
Jefferies, R., *The Toilers of the Field*, 1892.
Kent, N., *Hints to Gentlemen of Landed Property*, 1775.
Kilvert, F., *Journal of a Country Curate*, Cape, 1969.
King, G., *An Analysis of the Nation*, 1696.
Laurence, E., *The Duty and Office of a Land Steward*, 1727.
Le Balnc, J., *Letters on the English and French Nations*, 1747.
Loudon, J., *Encyclopaedia of Agriculture*, 1831.
Loudon, J., *Encyclopaedia of Cottage, Farm and Villa Architecture*, 1833.
MacKenzie, K. (trans.), Virgil's *The Georgics*, Folio Society, 1969.
Malden, W., *Farm Buildings*, 1896.
Marshall, W., *Rural Economy of Norfolk*, 1788.
Marshall, W., *Review of the County Reports to the Board of Agriculture*, 1818.
Melling, E., *Kentish Sources: Aspects of Agriculture and Industry*, Kent County Council, 1961.
Morton, J. C., *The Prince Consort's Farms*, 1863.
Newby, H., *Green and Pleasant Land*, 1978.
Papworth, J., *Rural Residences*, 1818.
Parker, R., *The Common Stream*, Collins, 1975.
Penoyre, J. and J., *Houses in the Landscape*, Faber, 1978.

Pike, M.(ed.), *Piddle Valley Book of Country Life*, Hutchinson, 1980.
Robinson, P., *Designs for Farm Buildings*, 1930.
Sainsbury, D., *Livestock Health and Housing*, Ballière Tindall, 1979.
Sayce, R., *Farm Buildings*, 1966.
Scott, J., *Farm Buildings: A Practical Treatise*, 1884
Shoard, M., *The Theft of the Countryside*, 1981.
Sinclair, J., *The Code of Agriculture*, 1831.
Stephens, H., and Burn, R., *The Book of Farm Buildings*, 1861.
Stephens, H., *Book of the Farm*, 1849 (and subsequent editions).
Thompson, F., *Lark Rise to Candleford*, Oxford University Press, 1945.
Thompson, F., *A Country Calendar*, edited M. Lane,
    Oxford University Press, 1979.
Tindall, G., *The Fields Beneath*, Granada, 1980.
Trevelyan, G., *English Social History*, Longmans, 1946.
Troubridge, R., *Farming Through the Ages*, Farming Press.
Trow-Smith, R., *A History of British Livestock Husbandry to 1700*, Routledge
    & Kegan Paul, 1957.
Tull, J., *The New Horse-Houghing Husbandry*, 1731.
Uttley, A., *The Country Child*, Faber, 1931.
Waistell, C., *Designs for Agricultural Buildings, Labourers' Cottages and
    Farm Houses*, 1827.
Waistell, C., *Treatise on the Arrangement of Agricultural Buildings*, 1851.
Whitlock, R., *A Short History of Farming in Britain*, Baker, 1965.
Williamson, H., *The Story of a Norfolk Farm*, Faber, 1941.
Williams, T., *Labour's Way to Use the Land*, 1935.
Winstanley, M., *Life in Kent*, Dawson, 1978.
Woodforde, J. *Diary of a Country Parson*, Oxford University Press, 1925.
Woodforde, J., *The Truth about Cottages*, Routledge & Kegan Paul, 1969.
Young, A., *On the Present State of the Waste Lands*, 1773.
Young, A., *General View of the Agriculture of Suffolk*, Kelley, 1978.
Young, A., *Tours*, Kelley.

Journals: *The Times, Country Life, Radio Times, RIBA Journal*.

Index

Model farm and workshops at Longleat,
Wiltshire, 1859 (Mansell Collection)

For Product Safety Concerns and Information please contact our EU
representative GPSR@taylorandfrancis.com
Taylor & Francis Verlag GmbH, Kaufingerstraße 24, 80331 München, Germany

www.ingramcontent.com/pod-product-compliance
Ingram Content Group UK Ltd.
Pitfield, Milton Keynes, MK11 3LW, UK
UKHW021827240425
457818UK00006B/99

* 9 7 8 1 0 3 2 5 4 2 0 7 2 *